Travel Agencies and Tourism Development

Travel Agencies and Tourism Development

B.S. Badan
Harish Bhatt

Commonwealth

Travel Agencies and Tourism Development

Edition : 2026

ISBN 81-311-0073-1

Published by :

COMMONWEALTH PUBLISHERS
4831/24, Prahlad Street,
Ansari Road, Darya Ganj,
New Delhi - 110002
Ph. : 23275511, 23257835
e-mail : commonwealthbooks@gmail.com

Typesetting by :
Rishu Computers
Delhi

Printed at :
Roshan Offset Printers
Delhi

Preface

Tourism can be defined as the act of travel for the purpose of recreation, and the provision of services for this act. It is a service industry, comprising a number of tangible and intangible components. The tangible elements include transportation systems—air, rail, road, water and now, space; hospitality services, accommodation, foods and beverages, tours, souvenirs; and related services such as banking, insurance and safety and security. The intangible elements include: rest and relaxation, culture, escape, adventure, new and different experiences.

Travel and tourism is a major industry in the world and is at the top of the league of invisible earners of foreign currency. Many sovereignties, along with their respective countries and states, depend heavily upon travel expenditures by foreigners as a source of taxation and income for the enterprises that sell services to these travellers. Consequently the development of tourism is often a strategy employed either by a non-governmental organization or a governmental agency to promote a particular region for the purpose of increasing commerce through exporting goods and services to non-locals.

During recent years the tourism industry has witnessed unprecedented growth. Increasing consumer demand for educational and participatory travel experiences has resulted in a variety of specialty niche markets such as ecotourism, cultural-heritage tourism, and agritourism. New paradigms link strategic tourism planning with sustainable development.

The leisure and tourism industry is one of the leading global economic activities, a multi-billion-dollar industry with

700 million international travellers per year around the world. Tourism is a motor for employment and income creation and, especially in poor countries, a vehicle for development. But today it is not sufficient to simply create employment without regard for the quality of jobs and the social and environmental effects of tourism in vulnerable areas. A growing number of organizations, including the tourism industry leadership, are increasingly conscious of the risks and are adopting a more responsible attitude.

The present publication provides an authoritative look at how to manage travel and tourism industry in a better way. It introduces the complexities of the tourism system so that they will be better positioned to eventually assume the managerial challenges and responsibilities in a diverse and challenging industry. The latest advancements in tourism theory and thinking, retaining the thoroughness of content, diversity of applications, regional and international issues, economic significance, tourism operators and the role of technology in the tourism industry etc. are also described elaborately. Numerous regional and global case studies and examples are included to provide an appropriately broad geographic context. This work will be highly informative and useful to students, researchers, policy makers, managers and working groups of travel and tourism industry.

B.S. Badan
Harish Bhatt

Contents

1

Introduction

Why do we refer to strategy as a *process*? The answer is that it is never a once for all event—it goes on and on. There is a need to continually review strategic objectives because the environment is always changing. The purpose of strategy is to make an organisation to fit into its environment. By achieving this, the probabilities that it will survive and prosper are enhanced. The first section of this book is concerned with introducing the subject matter of strategy in a specific context, namely that of travel and tourism. Thus in Part One concepts, definitions and the nature of objectives are discussed in Chapter 2 whilst Chapter 3 highlights the particular characteristics of travel and tourism which are relevant to understanding the way in which organisations within the industry are managed in a strategic way.

The subsequent parts of this book are concerned with examining the distinct 'stages' in the strategic process. It can be argued that strategy is a process because it contains distinct 'stages' and that there are three stages in all, as shown by Figure.

Strategic analysis

The purpose of strategic analysis is to gather information. None of us would be wise to make an important decision about anything in life without adequate and relevant information, and neither would a travel and tourism organisation.

There are two main stages in strategic analysis. First, strategic analysis involves an examination of an organisation's internal environment (*internal analysis*). This takes the form of a thorough analysis of the internal processes and structures of a business in much the same way as a doctor might carry out a thorough medical examination on a person. The purpose of internal analysis is to establish what the organisation is good at (its strengths) and what it is not so good at (its weaknesses).

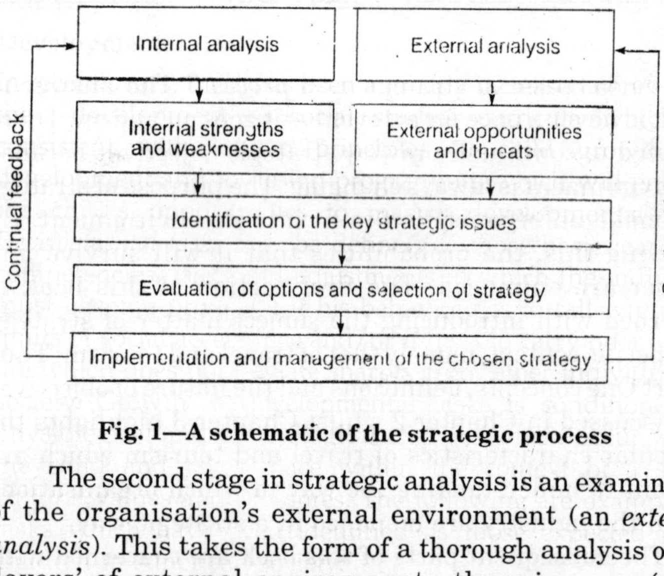

Fig. 1—A schematic of the strategic process

The second stage in strategic analysis is an examination of the organisation's external environment (an *external analysis*). This takes the form of a thorough analysis of two 'layers' of external environment—the micro—or 'near' environment and the macro- or 'far' environment. We will encounter the external environment in the book.

The macro-environment contains a range of influences that affect not only an organisation in an industry, but also the whole industry itself. It follows that a single organisation is usually unable to affect the factors in the macro-environment—successful strategy usually involves learning to cope and adapt to changes. This book explains the macro-environment in terms of five main areas of influence—socio-demographic, political, economic, environmental and technological influence.

The micro-environment comprises the industry in which the organisation competes. The organisation is usually affected by the factors in this environment and it may be able to have an influence upon it. However, unlike the internal environment the organisation does not have control over its micro-environment. We sometimes refer to the micro-environment as the competitive environment because it is within this sphere that an organisation competes, both for resource inputs and to sell its product outputs.

The information gathered from the external analysis, we seek to establish which influences represent opportunities, and which are, or might develop into, threats. Once we have established the organisation's internal strengths and weaknesses, and its external opportunities and threats, the challenge becomes to select a strategy that will address the weaknesses and threats whilst, at the same time, will build upon its strengths and exploit its opportunities. It is important to understand that a detailed internal and external analysis is a necessary prerequisite for the SWOT information—it emerges from the internal and external analysis.

The process sometimes involves an additional stage of condensing the strengths, weaknesses, opportunities and threats (SWOT) into a survey of the 'key issues'. These are the most pressing or most important elements of the SWOT statement—those which require the most urgent action or which the strategy should be particularly designed to address.

Strategic choice

The second stage in the strategic process involves taking the important information gathered from the strategic analysis and using it to make an intelligent and informed choice or selection of the most appropriate courses of action for the future. Choices are required about how the travel and tourism organisation (or its constituent parts) will compete, the strategic direction it will take and the methods which will be utilised.

It is at this stage that we come to appreciate the importance of the strategic analysis. If we have gained insufficient or flawed information from the analysis, then we cannot be sure that the strategy selection we make will be the right one.

Strategic choice therefore begins with an examination of the strategic analysis. Once we are acquainted with it, we normally generate a list of the options open to the organisation, paying particular attention to how each option will address the key issues. After this, we evaluate each option using a number of criteria. Finally, the most appropriate strategic option is selected.

Strategic implementation and management of change

The third stage in the strategic process involves taking the selected strategic option and actually putting it into practice.

This is a complex part of the process as it concerns putting detailed aspects of the strategy into practice. It involves *doing* the strategy and this brings into focus a number of other managerial issues. There are a number of areas of which we need to be aware in order to effectively implement a strategy for a travel and tourism organisation.

Implementation typically involves taking into account the following:

- the adequacy of the organisation's resource base;
- the readiness of the organisation's culture and structure to undertake the proposed strategy;
- the management of any changes that are needed to implement the strategy;
- the extent to which the organisation positions itself in respect to its geographic coverage and international presence.

In implementing the strategic process it is necessary to be aware not only of changes occurring to the internal and external environment, but also of changes to the subject matter itself. Thus Chapter considers the present and future trends occurring in the study of strategic management.

The 'feedback' link

Finally, the progress of strategy is monitored continually through feedback from the implementation stage back to the analysis stage. As a strategy proceeds, it may affect the organisation's internal environment and it may have an effect on the external environment. In addition, independent influences may have brought internal or external changes about since the strategic analysis was first carried out.

In order to ensure that the selected strategy is still appropriate, therefore, a review of the strategic analysis is necessary. If nothing has changed, then the company may decide that no amendment to the strategy is necessary. If the environment (internal or external) has changed, however, some modification to the strategy may become necessary.

2

Strategy and Strategic Objectives for Travel and Tourism Organisations

Introduction

Strategic thinking and strategic management are the most important activities undertaken by any business or public sector organisation. How skilfully these activities are carried out will determine the eventual long-term success or failure of the organisation. In this chapter, we introduce the most basic concepts in the study of these activities. The various definitions of the word *strategy* are discussed and then we explore the levels of decision-making in successful strategic management (at the strategic, tactical and operational levels). These are defined and the links between the levels are discussed. Finally, we discuss the nature of strategic objectives—who is responsible for setting them and what they are essentially about.

Learning Objectives

After studying this chapter, students should be able to:

- define the word *strategy* using Mintzberg's five Ps frame work;
- distinguish between deliberate (prescriptive) and emergent strategy;

- explain what strategy contains in practice;
- describe what is meant by *strategic*, *tactical* and *operational* decisions;
- explain what is meant by *hierarchical congruence* and why it is important;
- employ the stakeholder model to explain how strategic decisions are arrived at;
- define mission and describe the purpose and typical contents of a mission statement;
- explain the most typical types of objectives that are sought through strategic management.

What is strategy?

Definition

At the beginning of a book on strategy, the question 'What is strategy?' seems to be the most obvious starting point. The answer to the question is rather more complicated than it might at first appear. The growth of the subject has led to the use of the term strategy (and strategic management) in various ways.

Many organisations are hindered by short termism, concentrating on the most pressing immediate tasks at hand rather than looking ahead and taking a longer-term view. This is understandable given the pressures on modern business, but is not the most sensible way to manage. It is difficult to plan ahead (in the same way as it is difficult to forecast the weather) because there are so many sources of uncertainty and change, but concepts, frameworks, tools and techniques have been developed to facilitate the process. The overall aim of strategic management is thus to develop a framework for thinking ahead—for thinking strategically.

Historically, the term strategy has military roots, with commanders employing strategy in dealing with their opponents (see for example Keegan, 1988). Indeed, dictionaries often continue the military theme, defining strategy as 'the art of war'. Viewing strategy in such a way, the fundamental underlying premise of strategy becomes the notion that an adversary can be defeated (even a larger, more powerful one) if it can be outmanoeuvred using strategic skill.

Since the beginning of commercial transactions, businesses have had strategies determining their future courses of action. It is only since the 1960s, however, that the subject area has been widely considered as a topic of academic interest and hence widely taught in business schools and on business based courses. The subject is also widely taught as part of some tourism related courses and has received some attention in the tourism literature (see for example: Go and Pine, 1995; Hall, 2000; Holloway, 1998; Olsen *et al.*,1998; Phillips and Moutinho, 1998; Moutinho, 2000; Poon, 1993; Teare and Boer, 1991; Tribe, 1997).

As in the military arena so in business organisations attempt to outmanoeuvre their rivals. In so doing, strategies have to be developed that rely on various disciplines such as marketing, finance and human resource management.

. It is evident then, that people use the word *strategy* in different ways. You may have heard people talk about a strategy for a business, a strategy for a football match, a strategy for a military campaign or a strategy for revising for a set of exams. It was this multiplicity of uses of the term that led Henry Mintzberg at the McGill University in Montreal (Mintzberg, 1987) to propose his 'five Ps' of strategy.

Mintzberg's 'five Ps'

Mintzberg suggested that nobody can claim to own the word 'strategy' and that the term can legitimately be used in several ways. A strategy, he suggested, can be:

- a plan;
- a ploy;
- a pattern of behaviour;
- a position in respect to others;
- a perspective.

It is important not to see each of these Ps in isolation from each other. One of the problems of dividing ideas into frameworks like the five Ps is that they are necessarily simplified. The five Ps are not mutually exclusive, *i.e.* it is possible for an organisation to show evidence of more than one interpretation of strategy.

Plan strategies

A plan is probably the way in which most people use the word strategy. It tends to imply something that is intentionally put in train and its progress is monitored from the start to a predetermined finish. Some business strategies follow this model. 'Planners' tend to produce internal documents that detail what the company will do for a period of time in the future (say five years). It might include a statement on the overall direction that the organisation will take in seeking new business opportunities as well as a schedule for new product launches, acquisitions, financing (*i.e.* raising investment capital), human resource changes, etc.

A large tour operator, for instance, might decide that it plans to implement a strategy concerned with expanding its share of the market and that this will be achieved by setting prices at lower levels than competitors and by acquiring smaller firms. It might write its plans down in some detail and circulate them to all of its key managers so that, at any given point in time, the entire organisation can shown to be acting in accordance with the predetermined plan.

Ploy strategies

A ploy is generally taken to mean a short-term strategy, and is concerned with the detailed tactical actions that will be taken. It tends to have very limited objectives and it may be subject to change at very short notice. Mintzberg describes a ploy as, 'a manoeuvre intended to outwit an opponent or competitor' (Mintzberg *et al.*,1998: 14) He pointed out that some companies may use ploy strategies as threats. They may threaten to, say, decrease the price of their products simply to destabilize competitors.

One example of a ploy strategy is that employed in a soccer match. If the opposing team has a particularly skilful player, then the team manager may use the ploy of assigning two players to mark him for the duration of the game. However, this tactic will only last for the one game—the next game will have a completely different strategy. Furthermore, the strategy will only operate only as long as the dangerous player is on the pitch. If he is substituted or gets injured, the strategy will change mid-game.

Thus the tour operator (introduced above) may have an overall planned strategy which includes offering lower price levels than competitors, but as a short term ploy, it might suddenly discount its prices within six weeks of departure in order to destabilize its competitors and to sell excess capacity.

Pattern strategies

A 'pattern of behaviour' strategy is one in which progress is made by adopting a consistent form of behaviour. Unlike plans and ploys, patterns 'just happen' as a result of the consistent behaviour.

On a simple level, a small specialist tour operator offering summer villa and apartment holidays to a particular Greek island to a small but loyal group of customers might be viewed as following a pattern strategy. The company is unlikely to produce elaborate plans—simply renewing contracts with property owners and transport providers annually. If offered a new villa on favourable terms, then the operator would probably contract the property and feature it in its brochure without thinking much about it. It is an opportunity that is taken, as it appears too good to miss. However, the operator would probably not feature a hotel in Majorca although it may be available to the company because that would be outside their pattern of business behaviour.

Such patterns of behaviour are sometimes unconscious, meaning that they do not even realise that they are actually following a consistent pattern. Nevertheless, if it proves successful, it is said that the consistent behaviour has *emerged* into a success. This is in direct contrast to planning behaviour.

Deliberate and emergent strategies

There is a key difference between two of Mintzberg's Ps of strategy—plan and pattern. The difference is to do with the *source* of the strategy. He drew attention to the fact that some strategies are deliberate whilst others are emergent.

Deliberate strategy (sometimes called *planned* or *prescriptive* strategy) is meant to happen. It is preconceived, premeditated and usually monitored and controlled from start to finish. It has a specific objective.

Emergent strategy has no specific objective. It does not have a preconceived route to success BUT it may be just as effective as a deliberate strategy. By following a consistent pattern of behaviour, an organisation may arrive at the same position as if it had planned everything in detail.

Position strategies

A position strategy is appropriate when the important thing to an organisation is how it relates, or is positioned with respect to, its competitors or its markets (*i.e.* its customers). In other words, the organisation wishes to achieve or defend a certain position.

In business, companies tend to seek such things as market share, profitability, superior research, reputation, etc. It is plainly obvious that not all companies are equal when one considers such criteria. Some airlines, for instance, have enviable reputations for reliability and quality whilst others are not so fortunate. The competitors with a reputation to defend will use a position strategy to ensure that the reputation they enjoy is maintained and strengthened. This may even include marketing messages that point out the weaknesses in competitors' products whilst pointing out the features of their own.

Perspective strategies

Perspective strategies are about changing the culture (the beliefs and the 'feel', the way of looking at the world) of a certain group of people—usually the members of the organisation itself. Some companies want to make their employees think in a certain way, believing this to be an important way of achieving success. They may, for example, try to get all employees to think and act courteously, professionally or helpfully.

The elements of strategy

Chandler's definition

Given the foregoing definitions by Mintzberg, we might think that writers in business strategy are unable to agree on a single definition of the word strategy. This is partly true, but some have tried to sum it up succinctly to make it easier for students to understand. One such definition, still widely quoted, was offered by Professor Chandler of Harvard Business School in 1962. Given that Chandler predated Mintzberg, it is perhaps not surprising that it is rather more simplistic than Mintzberg might have accepted.

> Strategy is the *determination of the basic long-term goals* and objectives of an enterprise, and the adoption of *courses of action* and the *allocation of resources* necessary for carrying out these goals. (Chandler, 1962—emphasis added)

Three components of strategy

This is a useful definition because it shows the scope of what 'good' strategy is. The italics in this quote show the three important contents of strategy.

The *determination of the basic long-term goals* concerns the conceptualising of coherent and attainable strategic objectives. Without objectives, nothing else can happen. If you do not know where you want to go, how can you act in such a way as to get there?

The *adoption of courses of action* refers to the actions taken to arrive at the objectives that have been previously set. If, for example, your objective is arrive in London when travelling from Edinburgh there are various courses of action available to you. You might travel by train, by car, by coach or by plane. You might travel on certain days or at certain times of day. You might take advantage of certain concessionary fares, and you might make a booking through an intermediary such as a travel agent or book directly with the principal company (the airline or train company). Thus as a result of wanting to travel to London, a whole range of options need to be considered and detailed decisions have to be taken as to which options to select.

The *allocation of resources* refers to the fact that there is likely to be a cost associated with the actions required in order to achieve the objectives. If the course of action is not supported with adequate levels of resource, then the objective will not be accomplished.

Hence, strategy contains three things. In the example of travelling from Edinburgh to London:

1. Your *objective* is clearly stated as arriving in London at a certain date and time.
2. In order to achieve this objective certain *actions* are necessary. It is decided that flying is the best option. Thus a specified flight is booked through a travel agent, leave is taken from work and a plane is boarded at the airport.
3. However, the actions would not be possible if they could not be resourced. You need the *resources* of a plane with a suitably qualified pilot, an airport, money to pay for your flight and other such 'inputs'. If any one of these is missing, you will be unable to meet your objective.

Resources

Resource inputs (sometimes called *factors of production*) are those essential inputs that are essential to the normal functioning of the organisational process. These are the inputs, without which an organisation simply could not continue to exist or meet its objectives. We can readily appreciate that human beings rely upon certain vital inputs such as air, water, nutrition, warmth, shelter, etc., but organisations have similar needs. An organisation's resource inputs fall into four key categories:

1. *financial resources*—money for capital investment and working capital. Sources include shareholders, banks, bondholders, etc.
2. *human resources*—appropriately skilled employees to add value in operations and to support those that add value (*e.g.* supporting employees in marketing, accounting, personnel, etc.). Sources include the labour markets for the appropriate skill levels required by the organisation.
3. *physical (tangible) and operational resources*—land, buildings (offices, warehouses, etc.), plant, equipment, stock for production, etc. Sources include estate agents, builders, trade suppliers, etc.
4. *intellectual (intangible) resources*—inputs that cannot be seen or felt but which are essential for continuing business success. *e.g.* 'know-how', legally defensible patents and licences, brand names, registered designs, logos, 'secret' formulations and recipes, business contact networks, database, etc.

Levels of strategic decisions

Different 'levels'

It is useful at this stage to understand what characterizes strategic decisions. Management decisions within any organisation can be classified in three broad (and sometimes overlapping) categories: strategic, tactical and operation. These can be illustrated as a hierarchy in which higher level decisions tend to shape those at subordinate levels.

Strategic, tactical and operational decisions within an organisation differ from each other in items of:

- focus;
- the level in the organisation at which they are made;
- scope;
- time horizon;
- degree of certainty or uncertainty;
- complexity.

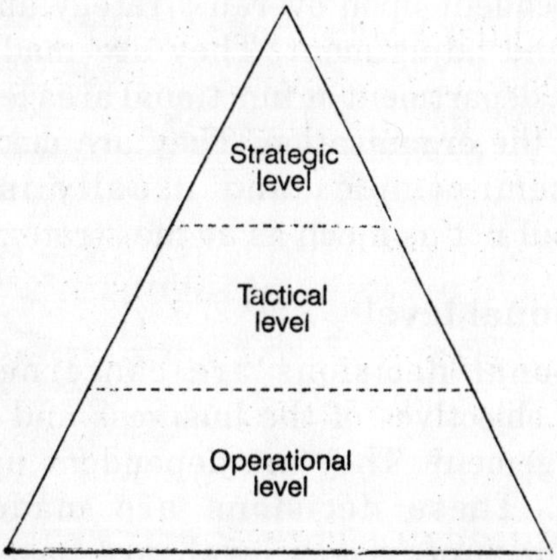

Fig. 2.1—Levels of strategic decision-making

The strategic level

Strategic decisions are concerned with the acquisition of sustainable competitive advantage which involves the setting of long-term corporate objectives and the formulation, evaluation, selection and monitoring of strategies designed to achieve those objectives. Strategic decisions are made by senior managers (usually directors), they affect the whole organisation, are long-term in nature, are complex and are based upon uncertain information. Managers at the strategic level require multiconceptual skills—the ability to consider the effects of multiple internal and external influences on the business and the possible ways in which strategy, can be adjusted to account for such influences.

The decision early on in the company's history for easy jet to operate as a low cost, no frills airline is an example of a strategic decision. It was taken at the most senior level, it affected the whole competitive position of the business, it was long-term in nature and it affected all members of the business.

The tactical level

Tactical decisions are concerned with how corporate objectives are to be met and how strategies are implemented.

They are dependent upon overall strategy and involve its fine-tuning and adjustment. They are made at head of business unit, department or functional area level and affect only parts of the organisation. They are medium-term in timescale, semi-complex and usually involve some uncertainty but not as much as at the strategic level.

The operational level

Operational decisions are concerned with the shorter-term objectives of the business and with its day to day management. They are dependent upon strategy and tactics. These decisions are made at junior managerial or supervisory level, are based on a high degree of certainty, and are not complex. The procedures in a sales office are typical operational activities—processing orders that have a tactical purpose in pursuit of the overall strategy.

Table 2.1 : Comparing strategic, tactical and operational decisions

	Strategic	Tactical	Operational
Focus of decision	Achieving sustainable competitive advantage	Implementation of strategy	Day-to-day operations
Level of decision making	Senior management, board of directors	Head of business unit or functional area	Supervisory
Scope	Whole organisation	Business unit or functional area (*e.g.* Marketing)	Department
Time horizon	Long-term (years)	Medium-term (months to years)	Short-term (days, weeks, month)
Certainty/ uncertainty	High uncertainty	Some uncertainty	High certainty
Complexity	Highly complex	Moderately complex	Comparatively simple
Examples	Decision to launch new product, enter new market, investment decision etc.	Decision to advertise, alter price etc.	Decision to re-order stock, scheduling of jobs

Congruency and 'fit'

The success of strategy rests upon a very important, but rather obvious principle. Once the strategic level objectives have been set, the operational objectives must be set in such a way so that they contribute to the achievement of the tactical and strategic objectives. In other words, the operational decisions must 'fit' the higher levels of decision-making. This introduces the concept of *congruence.*

The decision-making framework can be visualised as a pyramid (Figure 2.1). The top, where the strategic decisions are made, is thin whilst the bottom (operational decisions) is fatter. This representation is meant to show that strategic decisions are taken infrequently whilst operational decisions are taken often. Strategic decisions are few and far between whilst operational decisions are taken weekly, daily or even hourly. For every one strategic decision, there may be hundreds of individual operational decisions. Tactical decisions are between the two.

Time and planning horizons

One of the key differences between the three levels of decision-making in organisations is the timescale with which they are concerned. It is usually considered that the higher up the organisation, the longer the timescale with which management is concerned. Certainly this is true in most manufacturing companies, but in service companies where service delivery is of prime importance relatively senior staff can often be involved in operational decision making.

On an airline flight, for example, the flight crew, including the captain, are typically concerned with ensuring that the daily schedule runs safely and to time, whilst the chief executive may be worrying about potential threats that are some years away. Meanwhile, middle managers, say those in charge of graduate recruitment or the preparation of financial statements, will be planning a few months in advance—possibly as far as one year ahead.

Strategic management involves taking account of a large number of environmental variables. The longer ahead that a manager seeks to plan for, then the more uncertainty is introduced into the analysis.

Mission and mission statements

An organisation's *mission* can be described as its overarching *raison d'etre.* It is the objective that subsumes all others beneath it. For some organisations, the mission is very easy to articulate but for large commercial businesses, it tends to be more complex.

The purposes of a mission statement

Some organisations attempt to frame their mission in a formal statement, which is often to be seen adorning office walls, printed on employee identity cards and published in annual reports. Mission statements are commonly found both in the commercial sector and in the non-commercial (*not for profit*) sector. Such a statement has a number of possible purposes. It can be used to clearly communicate the objectives and values of the organisation to the various stakeholder groups and it can be argued that it assists in promoting hierarchical congruence. It may also have an effect in influencing the behaviour and attitudes of employees, although this is somewhat debatable as anecdotal evidence suggests that many employees have not in fact read their organisation's mission statement.

A mission statement can be seen as the starting point for an organisation's entire planning process since it requires senior management to sit down and seriously consider where the firm is and where it should be in the future. This point was emphasized by two leading management writers, when they stated that, 'in business like in art, what distinguishes leaders from laggards, and greatness from mediocrity, is the ability to uniquely imagine what could be' (Hamel and Prahalad, 1994: 25).

However, establishing an organisation's mission is not easy or without controversy, and as a result styles and content vary enormously. Drucker (1974: 94) pointed out that:

> defining the purpose and mission of the business is difficult, painful and riskiy. But it alone enables a business to set objectives, to develop strategies, to concentrate its resources and to go to work. It alone enables a business to be managed for performance.

Campbell and Yeung (1998) emphasized that whilst the mission statement itself is clearly important, it is also important for managers to instil a 'sense of mission' in employees. The success of the mission requires the behaviour of employees to match the values of the company, but such harmony is difficult to achieve and requires the mission as it is implemented to become embedded as part of the organisational culture.

Effective mission statements

- **Clearly articulated.** The mission statement should be simple to comprehend so that employees and other stakeholders can clearly understand the principles and values that will guide them in their dealings with the organisation. The statement must be specific enough to have an impact upon the behaviour of individuals.
- **Relevant.** The mission statement should be appropriate to the organisation in terms of its history, culture and shared values. The mission should not be too broad or too narrow. Too broad may result in lack of focus. Too narrow may mean factors that are potentially important to the organisation will be overlooked.
- **Current.** An unchanged mission statement may no longer be able to act as a driving force guiding the organisation into the future.
- **Positive tone.** The mission statement should be written in such a way that encourages commitment and energizes or inspires employees.

- **Individuality.** The mission statement should set it apart from other organisations establishing its individuality it not its uniqueness through an emphasis on the advantages of the organisation based on an objective assessment of organisational strengths and weaknesses.
- **Enduring.** The mission statement cannot be continually altered, as this would be confusing, so they are likely to remain in place for a number of years. Consequently they must be written to allow for some flexibility.
- **Adapted.** Mission statements are written with various target audiences in mind, some for employees only, some for shareholders and other external groups, and others for all audiences. The information and style should reflect the relevant target audience.

Source: Adapted from Stone (1996)

What does a mission statement contain?

The style, content and terminology of mission statements vary enormously. Some are long and detailed whereas others are short and to the point. Some are focused on a particular audience (such as employees or customers) others are written with multiple target audiences in mind. There are probably no 'rights' or 'wrongs' of how it should be presented or what it should contain it all depends upon the organization and its culture. In assessing mission statements the reader will find many examples of the use of language that is ambiguous in its meaning or is questionable in its use of 'hype' to inflate the image of the organization. In practice, mission statements usually contain one or more of the following:

- Some *indication of the industry* or business the organization is mainly concerned with.
- An indication of the *realistic market share* or market position the organisation should aim towards.
- A brief summary of the *values and beliefs* of the organisation in relating to key stakeholder groups such as customers and employees.

- An indication of the *ownership* or control of the organisation.
- A summary of the *geographical location* or scope of organisational activities.
- Specific and *highly context-dependent objectives* are sometimes expressed in the mission statement.

A selection of mission statements taken from a range of tourism organisations in various sectors of the industry is presented below.

British Airways

British Airways introduced a new mission statement after a consultation process involving employees in 1997. The mission statement replaced an existing statement which had been drawn up in 1995 in the run-up to privatisation, and many employees have received training in its meaning for their particular jobs. In introducing its new mission British Airways cited four vital challenges for change facing the company:

- What customers are asking for?
- What people want?
- The global economic climate.
- The challenge of competition.

'Whatever it is called, a vision, mission or strategic intent, its purpose is to provide a guiding light for the future. Companies without a mission are prone to opportunism, incrementalism, to constant changes of direction, to being driven by short-term budgetary pressures and to corporate confusion.

A unifying mission is especially important in large companies where staff and managers are expected to take decisions themselves, without constant referral back to headquarters or to their seniors. If everyone understands where the company is aiming, then independent decisions are more likely to be aligned with each other and with the companies' ultimate objective.

A mission also helps an organisation set stretching goals and then drive its short-term plans and budgetary trade-offs to achieve the long-term aim.'

Source: British Airways News, 2 May, 1997

British Airways Mission Statement Post 1997

OUR MISSION

'To be the undisputed leader in world travel'.

We are passionately committed to excellence and to the highest levels of customer service.

OUR GOALS

Customers' Choice—Airline of first choice in our key markets.

Strong Profitability—Meeting investors' expectations and securing the future.

Truly Global—Global network, global Outlook: recognised everywhere for superior value in world travel.

Inspired People—Inspired teams of people, building and benefiting from the company's success.

OUR VALUES

Safe and Secure

Honest and Responsible

Innovative and Team-spirited

Global and Caring

A Good Neighbour

Source: British Airways Fact Book 1999

British Airways Mission Statement Pre 1997

OUR MISSION

'To be the best and most successful company in the airline business'.

OUR GOALS

Safe and Secure—To be a safe and secure airline.

Financially strong—To deliver strong and consistent financial performance.

Global leader—To secure a leading share of air travel business world-wide with a significant presence in all major geographical markets.

Service and Value—To provide overall superior service and good value for money in every market segment in which we compete.

Customer driven—To excel in anticipating and quickly responding to customer needs and competitor activity.

Good employer—To sustain a working environment that attracts, retains and develops committed employees who share in the success of the company.

Good neighbour—To be a good neighbour, concerned for the community and the environment.

FOUR KEY OBJECTIVES

To be genuinely the world's favourite airline.

To be pre-eminent in customer service.

To be truly global.

To be the UK's best managed company by the year 2000.

Source: British Airways Fact Book 1996

Southwest Airlines

The mission of Southwest Airlines is dedication to the highest quality of customer service delivered with a sense of warmth, friendliness, individual pride and company spirit.

To Our Employees

We are committed to provide our Employees a stable work environment with equal opportunity for learning and personal growth. Creativity and innovation are encouraged for improving the effectiveness of Southwest Airlines. Above all, Employees will be provided the same concern, respect and caring attitude within the organisation that they are executed to share externally with every Southwest Customer.

Source: www.southwest.com

Maldives Tourism Promotion Board

VISION

- Be the most exclusive destination in South Asia.
- Be the top tourism earner in South Asia.
- Be an example of sustainable tourism development in small island nations.

MISSION

The Maldives Tourism Promotion Board will promote quality and sustainable growth in the tourism industry of the Maldives to foster a well utilised and financially healthy private sector industry—in this way enabling the industry to deliver long-term economic, social and cultural benefits to the people of the Maldives, whilst at the same time contributing to enhancements to the Maldives' unspoiled marine environment to the benefit of the people and visitors of the Maldives.

OBJECTIVES

- To strengthen and enhance the exclusive image of the destination in the source markets.
- To position the Maldives as the 'premium' destination world-wide.
- To achieve growth targets set for the destination in the Marketing Plan for each year.
- To diversify the source markets as well as the market segments to the destination.
- To undertake market research to monitor the world economic conditions and travel trends in order to identify market opportunities.
- To monitor and support the private sector in their operations to maintain viable bed occupancy levels and to iron out seasonal fluctuations in visitor arrivals.

Source: www.visitmaldives.com

Holidaybreak plc

Holidaybreak is the UK's leading operator of specialist holiday businesses. Group companies retain a distinctive identity whilst sharing expertise and exploiting opportunities in areas of common interest.

Our aim is to achieve continuing profitable growth by developing our existing businesses and market leading brands in the UK and European holiday markets and through acquisitions in the travel sector.

Certain core values will be common to all:

- High levels of customer service.
- Excellent value for money for all customers.
- An open and cooperative working environment where individual initiative and responsibility are encouraged.
- A commitment to the welfare and development of all employees.
- The maintenance of good supplier relations.
- Continuous improvement in everything we do.

Source: www.holidaybreak.co.uk

How do businesses set objectives?

Earlier in this chapter, we introduced the idea that strategic objectives, since they represent the most important level of decision-making, are set by an organisation's senior management, usually the board of directors. In setting objectives, however, senior managers are likely to be influenced by a range of different groups, which have an interest in the organisation. *Who or what influences the senior management in their objective-setting?* This question cuts to the heart of an important debate that is taking place both in universities and in business circles. This debate revolves around two differing approaches towards objective-setting: the stockholder and stakeholder approaches.

The stockholder approach

The stockholder approach argues that businesses exist primarily for their owners (usually shareholders). Accordingly, any business behaviour that renders profit performance sub-optimal is not only theft from shareholders but will also, eventually, lead to a level of business performance that will harm all other groups such as employees, customers and suppliers.

In 1970, the Nobel Laureate Professor Milton Friedman contended that 'the moral obligation of business is to increase its profits'. Friedman argued that the one and only obligation of company directors (which are the legal agents of shareholders' financial interests) is to act in such a way as to maximize the financial rate of return on the owners' shares. The capitalist system upon which the Western economies rests in large part upon the presupposition that investments made in shares (*e.g.* in pension funds, unit trusts, etc.) will perform well. The profitable performance of shares lies in an increase in the share's value and in the rate of dividend per share—objectives that can only be served by financial profits.

The stakeholder approach

A stakeholder can be defined as:

> *Any group or individual who can affect or is affected by the achievement of an organisation's objectives.* (Freeman, 1984: 46)

This definition draws in almost everybody that is, or may be potentially involved in the life of an organisation. It consequently goes without saying that not all stakeholders are equal in their influence on an organisation's objectives.

The stakeholder approach (as advocated by Freeman, 1984; Donaldson and Preston, 1995 and Campbell, 1997a), argues that organisations, like individual people, are characterised by their relationships with various groups and individuals such as employees and customers. A group or individual qualifies as a stakeholder if it/he/she has a legitimate interest in the organisation's activities and thus has the power to affect the firm's performance and/or has a stake in the firm's performance.

The implications of this proposition are far-reaching. In essence, stakeholder theory argues that shareholders are neither the sole owners of a business nor the sole beneficiaries of its activities. Whilst shareholders are undeniably one stakeholder group, they are far from being the only group who expect to benefit from business activity and, accordingly, are just one of those groups who have a legitimate right to influence a company's strategic objectives. Some of these groups are internal to the organisation whilst others are external. Stakeholder groups, which might be able to exert an influence over the setting of objectives, are shown in Table 2.2.

Table 2.2—Examples of internal and external stakeholders

Internal stakeholders	External stakeholders
Board of directors	Shareholders
Employees collectively	Creditors (existing and potential)
Individual employees (*e.g.* founding entrepreneur)	Suppliers (existing and potential)
Employees' representatives (trade unions, trade associations etc.)	Customers (existing and potential)
Functional business areas (marketing, finance etc.)	Trade bodies (*e.g.* ABTA)
Geographical areas of the organisation (*e.g.* Europe, Asia etc.)	Pressure groups (*e.g.* environmental)
	Competitors (current and future, national and international)
	Government (legal, fiscal and regulatory impacts)
	Private individuals
	International regulatory bodies (*e.g.* IATA)
	The local community

Stakeholders and objectives

One widely used and useful model for understanding how stakeholders exert influence on an organisation's objectives was proposed by Mendelow (1991). According to this model, stakeholders can be 'ranked' depending upon two variables: *interest* and *power:*

- stakeholder *power* refers to the *ability* to influence the organisation;
- stakeholder *interest* refers to the *willingness* to influence the organisation.

In other words, interest concerns the extent to which the stakeholder cares about what the organisation does.

It then follows that:

Stakeholder influence = power × interest

The actual influence that a stakeholder has will depend upon where the stakeholder is positioned with respect to ability to influence and willingness to influence. A stakeholder with both high power and high interest will be more influential than one with low power and low interest. We can map stakeholders by showing the two variables on a grid comprising two intersecting continua (Fig. 2.2).

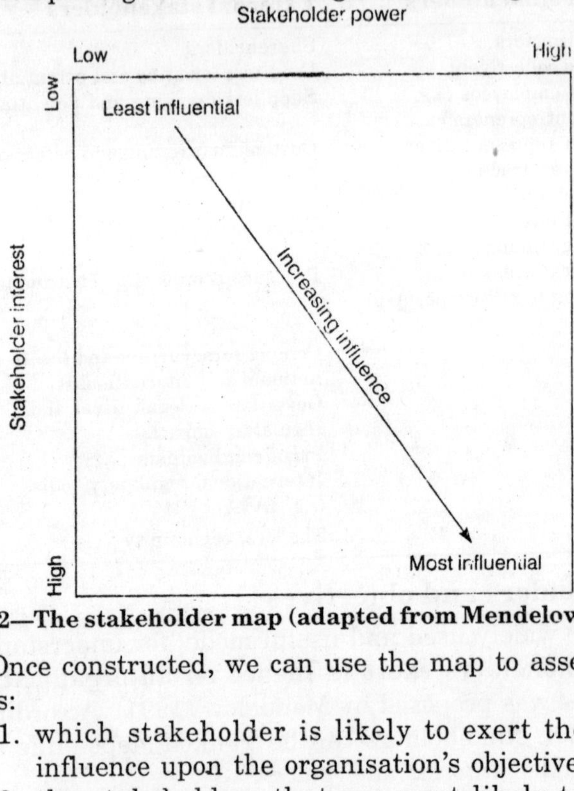

Fig. 2.2—The stakeholder map (adapted from Mendelow, 1991)

Once constructed, we can use the map to assess two things:

1. which stakeholder is likely to exert the most influence upon the organisation's objectives, and;
2. the stakeholders that are most likely to be in potential conflict over strategic objectives (where two or more stakeholders are in close proximity in the high power—high interest part of the map).

The managing director and the board of directors are examples of stakeholders with both high power and high interest. This is because they manage the business, depend upon it for their jobs and their positions within the organisation give them power with which to implement their decisions. The local community (in most cases) will not concern itself with the setting of organisational objectives and have limited power to impose their views.

The content of corporate objectives

The importance of objectives

In strict terms, the most important of all objectives is simply to survive as a going concern. Other objectives depend upon the type of organisation and the nature of its environment. Objectives are not necessarily mutually exclusive in that an organisation can usually pursue more than one type of objective at the same time. Juach and Glueck (1988) defined an objective as 'the end the firm seeks and the criteria the firm uses to determine its effectiveness'. The objectives can be written in a *closed* manner in that they are stated in quantitative terms and are specific in relation to form and timescale, or an *open* manner in that they are stated in qualitative terms and are general in form and timescale.

Objectives are essential to the successful accomplishment of the managerial function in any formal organisation in that they:

- provide a sense of direction;
- provide a standard of measurement and a means of controlling performance;
- project an image of the organisation's style.

Corporate objectives

Corporate objectives translate the mission into specific long-term targets that can usually be quantified and measured. Corporate objectives are strategic level objectives that can be used as a starting point in the setting business (or tactical) and operational objectives which are more detailed objectives set lower down the organisational hierarchy (see the foregoing discussion). The business objectives will usually relate to important constituent parts of the overall organisation— often termed strategic business units (SBUs), whilst the operational objectives will usually relate to smaller units or teams within each SBU.

Corporate objectives normally:

- relate to the whole organisation;
- apply to the medium to long term;*
- are set by senior management;
- relate to a number of key areas of concern;
- can be pursued simultaneously.

Care must be taken in writing corporate objectives so that they are clear and easily understood. A common view is that objective writing is a *'CRIME'* in that corporate objectives should be:

- *Communicable*—capable of being easily communicated down the line to the workforce and other internal and external stakeholder groups.
- *Realistic*—capable of being achieved within the timescale.
- *Internally consistent*—consistent with the overall organisational mission, the operational objectives and the strategy for achieving the objectives set.
- *Measurable*—capable of being quantified so that they can be measured and it is possible to assess whether the objectives have been achieved.
- *Explicit*—written in clear unambiguous language, precise in relation to both targets set and to timescale.

Corporate objectives often relate to economic and social concerns and to matters of growth and competitive advantage which will now be considered.

---

* Note time horizons vary considerably and will depend largely upon the nature of the business, especially the lead time taken to launch new products and services. In some industries such as pharmaceuticals and chemicals where heavy capital expenditure is required and where research and development are time-consuming, lead times may be long. In many sectors of travel and tourism lead times will be comparatively short, since launching a new destination or a new route for example can be achieved fairly quickly. However, where large capital investment is required, as with hotel construction or new aircraft purchases, lead times are likely to be quite long. As a working rule the long term is often considered to be 5+years, the medium term 1+5 years and the short term less than 1 year.

Economic objectives

Economic objectives are those that can be measured in financial ways. For commercial organisations, objectives will usually include measures such as *return.* Return is an accounting term to describe the proportion of either sales or investment capital that is left over as profit. In commercial organisations the economic objective is often referred to as the *primary objective,* with other objectives being *secondary* to the achievement of the financial objectives.

Return on sales, sometimes referred to as profit margin, is an indication of how well the company has controlled its costs whilst *return on assets* (or *return on capital employed*) is an indication of how efficiently the company has used its investors' money. Both of these are important business objectives—to provide sufficient return to retain some profits for future investment and to provide investors with a dividend on their shareholding.

Not-for-profit organisations also have economic objectives but they are measured in different ways. Organisations like destination marketing offices, charities and government departments tend to measure economic performance by using cost—benefit or value-for-money objectives. These organisations usually rely in large part on income over which they have little control—it may, for example, be fixed by central or local government. The objectives set will typically involve extracting the maximum benefit in terms of outputs from the income they have.

A destination marketing office for a country, a city or a resort for example, will have a certain income which it uses as carefully as possible to ensure it can deliver as many tourists of required type as possible to the destination within its allocated budget.

Social objectives

We should not assume that all organisational objectives are financial in nature. Many exist, either in part or totally, to deliver social benefits. Many publicly funded organisations such as museums, art galleries, heritage attractions and so on exist to deliver services to society in general. Charities exist primarily to provide social benefit to one or more allegedly worthwhile constituencies. For organisations of this type, economic objectives may be secondary to their desire to deliver socially desirable ends.

Commercial organisations are also gradually adopting social objectives in their strategic planning. Although they are usually subordinate to their economic objectives, commercial organisations may espouse social or environmental causes that they purport to believe in. They may, for example, recognise the social value of supporting local community projects or seconding (at their own expense) some of their people to serve with charities.

Growth or market share objectives

At some stages in the life of an organisation, objectives concerning growth and expansion become among the most important. This is especially true of businesses who must grow and maintain market position in order to 'keep up with' or 'keep ahead of' competitors.

Size and market position offer a number of advantages and it is these that an organisation seeks when growth is a key objective. Size gives an organisation economy of scale advantages in both product and resource markets. It means that a larger organisation attracts resource inputs at preferential unit cost compared to smaller concerns and its larger presence in its product markets increases its pricing power and its ability to subjugate competitors.

Competitive advantage objectives

Finally, and importantly, many strategic objectives concern the company's position in respect to its competitors. Competitive advantage objectives concern how the company's position compares to others—especially to competitors. The objectives are limited to ensuring simply that 'we beat you', or 'we are better than you'. Superior performance is the only objective and if a company can achieve ascendancy over its nearest competitors, then the objective will have been accomplished.

Objectives in British Airways

An illustration of the cascading of objectives is provided by British Airways.

The mission sets the long-term direction, which is used to identify the strategic goals needed to achieve the mission. The mission and strategic goals provide a planning horizon of 10 years between 1997 and 2007. The combined mission and corporate goals is provide the parameters and relevance for 3-year business plans for each of the key areas of business (the SBUs), which in turn are used to set each year's budget for each department. The business plan and budget determine the actions required by each department which in turn determine individuals' work programmes. Relevant key performance indicators (KPI) are set for each individual employee.

Source: Adapted from *British Airways News,* 2 May 1997

3

Introduction to Strategy for Travel and Tourism

Introduction

Travel and tourism strategy represents a key challenge to managers because of the nature of the products being sold and of the complexities of the environment in which the industry exists. In particular, however, strategy is informed by the fact that most travel and tourism products are services rather than goods (*i.e.* they are intangible). In this chapter, we consider how the nature of a travel and tourism product informs strategy formulation, both in a general sense (because they are mainly intangible) and in a more specific discussion of the products themselves.

Learning Objectives

After studying this chapter, students should be able to:

- define goods and services;
- explain the product features of travel and tourism products;
- describe the key features of service products and how they relate to travel and tourism;
- describe six product factors that specifically apply to travel and tourism.

Travel and tourism as a service industry

Goods and services

In a book such as this on travel and tourism strategy, it is appropriate to define the products that comprise the central themes that we will be studying. If you have studied business or economics before, you will remember that there are two basic types of product—goods and services. Goods are tangible—things you can own, whilst services are intangible and are things done on your behalf or for your benefit. You do not 'own' service products but instead you have use of them. For example, as a customer you do not own an aircraft seat on a flight or a cruise ship you may be travelling on but you make use of the services offered.

Travel and tourism products have a number of characteristics which are of relevance to the way in which they are managed. These characteristics are discussed in the following section. Whilst some of these features are common to all service products, some other characteristics are unique to travel and tourism products.

Service product characteristics

Characteristics of service products

There are a number of factors which make services different from physical goods. These distinguishing factors are:

- intangibility;
- inseparability;
- perishability;
- heterogeneity;
- ownership.

We will consider each characteristic in turn.

Intangibility

Services cannot normally be seen, touched, smelt, tasted, tried on for size or stored on a shelf prior to purchase. Their intangibility makes them harder to buy but easier to distribute.

The fact that the tourism product is not a physical object but an amalgam of 'invisible' services does create certain problems for organisations operating in the sector. To overcome this intangibility, tour operators sometimes attempt to create some form of tangible offering that potential customers can relate to. With the growth in the home ownership of video-recorders and computers for example, tour operators and destinations are now able to record the features of their holidays on video or make them available on the Internet for home viewing by potential customers. This takes away some of the uncertainty the customer may have when buying a holiday. Similarly, travel brochures help to overcome the intangibility problem and this is why so much effort, expense and creativity are devoted to their design.

Key concept: Packages and tour operators

A 'package' can be defined as a pre-arranged combination, sold or offered for sale at an inclusive price, of not less than two of the following three elements:

- transport;
- accommodation;
- other tourist services not ancillary to transport or accommodation and accounting for a significant part of the package.

The growth of the package has been a major cause of the increase in the holiday market since the 1950s. The role of the package company goes beyond that of the wholesaler, in that they not only purchases or reserve the separate components in bulk but, in combining these components into an 'inclusive tour', they also become producers in the holiday market. The traditional appeal of the tour operators' product has been to offer a complete holiday package at the lowest price to a population often lacking the linguistic knowledge or the knowledge and confidence to organise independent travel. Consequently the tour operation has become the dominant feature of the holiday market in many tourist-generating countries.

Inseparability

The production and consumption of services are inseparable. To take advantage of an air flight or a bus service, for example, both you and the means of transport must make the journey at the same time. The implication of this inseparability is that the consumers have direct experience of the production of the service. They are, in effect, in the 'service factory' at the time of production. This has profound implications for the staff in service industries.

When a physical product is purchased, it comes packaged and the customer is likely to assess the product purely upon its product features (such as taste, size, specification, etc.). Managers have time to plan these aspects of product management to ensure that customer satisfaction is achieved. The circumstances under which the product is produced and how it is delivered are usually of little relevance to the customer.

In the case of a service product, however, customers are likely to be very concerned about the way in which the product is delivered, *i.e.* the level of customer service. At a hotel reception desk, for example, the customer is likely to notice if the receptionist is rude or unwelcoming. Similarly, the customer will also experience the production of the product if the receptionist is efficient, courteous and helpful.

The task of satisfying customers for the provider of a service is in many ways much more difficult than it is for the manufacturer of a product. In service industries everything has to be right first time, all the time and any mistake can prove very costly in terms of lost future custom. How service personnel conduct themselves in the customer's presence, what they say, what they don't say, how competent they are, how personable they are or how presentable they are, can determine whether the customer buys from the business again.

Perishability

Since production and consumption are simultaneous, services are instantly perishable if they have not been sold at the time of the production. The empty train seat, the empty hotel bed or the unsold holiday all represent lost opportunities. They are lost sales that can never be recovered (empty hotel rooms cannot be 'stored' for when demand increases). Unlike manufacturers of goods, they cannot just keep on producing services and store them for future sales and striking the correct balance between capacity and sales (supply and demand) is extremely difficult.

Consumer Capacity, Occupancy for accomodation

In travel and tourism, capacity refers to the number of people that can be accommodated in a hotel, aircraft, bus, resort, etc. It may be, for example, that a hotel has a capacity of 300 and an aircraft might be able to accommodate 130.

The important figure, however, is how much of the capacity is actually used at any time. This is the occupancy rate for accommodation or the load factor for transportation. If a hotel, for example, is only full on a quarter of the nights in a year, then it is paying the fixed costs on the empty rooms without any income from them. This is particularly important when considering seasonality and also explains why hotel prices fall in the low season—to maintain as high an occupancy rate as possible to help to cover the hotel's total costs.

The problems of perishability can be made even more acute by fluctuating demand but fixed supply. Demand can vary during the day, during the week or from season to season of the year. Many resort hotels, for instance, are full for only a few months of the year. Capacity may therefore be insufficient to meet demand at peak times, but in excess of what is required at slack times.

Demand can fluctuate for all sorts of reasons, such as seasonal changes, changes due to the level of economic activity, and changes due to climatic conditions. Changes in demand can also occur very suddenly and can have a dramatic impact on service suppliers. For instance a single reported terrorist attack in a destination area could severely limit demand. Or more widespread instability such as the Gulf War of 1991 can also curtail demand. In the case of the

Gulf War, the airline industry worldwide faced a major downturn in demand.

Supply, however is much more difficult to alter, at least in the short term. For example, a hotel has a fixed bedstock (number of beds) that it has to try to fill. A scheduled airline has an obligation to fly between advertised points regardless of the number of empty seats on the aircraft. A tour operator enters a contractual obligation, often months in advance of the date of travel, with the providers of accommodation to fill a certain specified number of rooms.

The management challenges, therefore, is to make sure that the company is operating at full capacity for a much of the time as possible. To be successful, the company will need carefully designed strategies to stimulate demand, lengthen seasons, or to offer appropriate pricing levels to manage and 'smooth out' occupancy levels.

Heterogeneity

Services, unlike mass-produced manufactured, goods, are never identical. One hotel in a chain of hotels, or one person's holiday, will never be identical to another. The human element and other factors in delivering services, ensures that services will be heterogeneous, *i.e.* varied.

Tourism products are 'people oriented', and the human factor plays a key role. The enjoyment gained from a holiday cannot be separated from the personalities who go to make up that holiday—the personnel employed in the travel agency, the airline crew, the hotel, staff, the tour operator's overseas representative, and of course, the holidaymaker. All of these have a role to play in ensuring that the holiday lives up to the customer's expectations.

Human behaviour, however, is highly variable and it is difficult for a company to ensure that its employees display good customer relation skills all of the time. Similarly, the company has no influence over the behaviour of the customer when on holiday. the customer's attitudes and behaviour will also contribute to the pleasure gained from the holiday. This means that there is an uncontrollable element inherent in the production of the travel or tourism product which can lead to the holidaymaker being satisfied or disappointed with the holiday.

To take account of this problem, it is important that as much information as possible is provided in advance to the potential customer, both by the tour operator and the travel agent. This will reduce the risk of the customer purchasing an unsuitable holiday at the outset. Special attention has also to be paid to the personnel who will deal with the client on a face-to-face basis to make certain that they have suitable personalities for dealing with the public.

In many cases in travel and tourism, the customer is actually attracted by the heterogeneity. Tourists would become bored if every tourist destination was identical, and hotel chains try hard to maintain a consistent brand image whilst at the same time trying to differentiate each hotel through varying design features. This heterogeneity is understandable, but it does make it very difficult for potential purchases to evaluate services and for managers to deliver products of a consistent quality.

Managing 'heterogeneity' at Radisson Hotels International

Radisson Hotels is part of the privately owned Carlson group of companies based in Minneapolis. Other companies in the group include a leading US travel agency chain and the international Carlson Wagonlit business travel agencies. Radisson has grown rapidly in recent years, despite problems elsewhere in the hotel sector because it focused on management contracts and franchising in its hotels rather than in real estate investment, *i.e.* another party owns the physical structure of the hotels. The company has concentrated on its strengths in management, marketing and sales. The company has some 400 hotels with 97000 rooms, in 53 countries. Radisson owns very few of these hotels and manages about 50 while the rest are franchised, *i.e.* they are managed by franchisees operating in partnership with Radisson.

Radisson's goal is to be the fastest growing quality hotel chain, seeking to operate in the upmarket business travel and leisure destination markets. It relies on a variety of upmarket products, including deluxe Plaza hotels, all-suite hotels, inns and resorts. Plans for future development call for targeting Europe (especially eastern Europe), Asia Pacific, the Caribbean, South America and Canada.

The challenges for a company such as Radisson include ensuring that the same levels of quality are provided around the world, when:

- staff come from many cultural and linguistic backgrounds;
- locations vary greatly in their geographical characteristics;
- the company does not actually own the buildings.

The strength of a brand such as Radisson relies upon such standards being ensured, but in practice it is a very difficult management task, since even communicating effectively with worldwide locations in different time zones can be problematic.

Radisson relies heavily on alliances with local 'quality' hoteliers, places a great emphasis on training, standardizes procedures where possible, carefully words all its management and franchising agreements, and has sophisticated international communications including its 'Pierre' transcontinental toll-free reservations services.

Ownership

When a customer buys a manufactured product there will usually be a document, such as a receipt, which transfers ownership from seller to buyer. When a consumer buys a service he or she does not usually receive ownership of anything tangible. A car is hired, but ownership is not transferred, a hotel room is reserved for a period of time but nothing in it is ever owned by the customer. Even a credit card actually remains the property of the issuing company.

Service buyers are therefore buying only access to or use of something, which has important management implications. Since transfer of ownership is not involved the task of building a relationship with customers, of retaining their custom, and building brand loyalty become more difficult.

Travel and tourism-specific characteristics of service

Six travel and tourism-specific factors

The five special characteristics of services cited in the preceding section change the emphasis of a manager's task when compared to the sale of goods. However, these characteristics, whilst applicable to the travel and tourism industry, are not unique to it but could be applied to other service sectors.

Six further factors, however, might be added in the travel and tourism context:

1 High cost,
2 Seasonality,
3 Ease of entry/exit,
4 Interdependence,
5 Impact on society,
6 The effect of external shocks.

Whilst these factors are not unique to travel and tourism, they are certainly very important to any consideration of strategic management in a travel and tourism context.

The fifth of these factors, tourism's impact on society, is unique to the industry, in that no other service industry can claim to have such a visible impact which can be highly significant in the way in which organisations and destinations are managed. Finally, managing in the travel and tourism industry is carried out at the mercy of events.

High cost

Travel and tourism products usually represent a relatively high cost purchase for the consumer. Taking a holiday, buying an airline ticket or staying at a hotel are expensive. Indeed in some cases such purchases will represent the largest single item of expenditure for a consumer in a given year. Consequently, making such a purchase does not usually occur without a great deal of thought and a comparison of alternation offerings. It is not like buying a fast moving consumer good, which may be done on impulse. This feature of travel and tourism products is important when formulating strategy, especially with regard to marketing.

Seasonality

Bull (1995) argued that 'Tourism has one of the most highly seasonal patterns of demand for any product, having less variation than the demand for Christmas cards or air conditioners, but more than nearly all high value individual purchases'. This seasonality has implications for the price and quantity of tourism products supplied between seasons. One way in which management can respond to these problems of seasonality is to develop or acquire counter-seasonal business, *i.e.* to develop from their own resources or to purchase business that operate primarily at other times of the year.

Table 3.1— Example of seasonal market for air travel: economy class excursion fares London-Sydney 1994/95

Season	Period of application	Fare (UK £)	Index
Basic	16 Apr. - 15 June	860	100
Off-peak	01 Feb. - 15 Apr. 16 Jun. - 31 Jul.	1045	122
Shoulder	01 Aug. - 09 Dec. 25 Dec. - 31 Jan.	1245	145
Peak	09 Dec. - 24 Dec.	1400	163

Source: Bull (1995), based on IATA 1994 Air Tariffs/Galileo CRS

Table 3.1 shows the four different seasonal markets for air travel between London, UK and Sydney, Australia which have developed over a number of years with prices varying by up to 63%.

Managing variations in seasonal demand at First Choice Holidays plc

First Choice Plc is the UK's fourth largest outbound tour operator, with about 13% of the total Air Inclusive Tour or 'package' (AIT) market. The JK AIT market is highly seasonal, being concentrated in the months of June, July and August and with almost 50% of customers choosing Spain as their holiday destination.

Such seasonality of demand causes some managerial problems:

- Profits are concentrated in the second half of the financial year, and losses usually incur for the first 6 months. First Choice lost £39.7 million in the six months to the end of April 2001, but recorded a profit of £79.6 million in the full financial year to October, 2001. Such uneven performances can make the financial markets uneasy and this, in turn, can make it more difficult to raise new finance.
- Large fluctuations in cash flow occur. Typically cash flows in during the early part of the calendar year as bookings are made and paid for, but then cash is drained over the course of the summer months as the companies have to pay accommodation, airline and other expenses. Net cash levels are usually at their lowest levels during the autumn and early winter. Many companies have to rely on bank borrowing facilities to support them during this period and some companies have failed due to banks' refusal to support AIT companies through their cash deficit months.
- 'Integrated' travel companies such as My Travel and First Choice own charter airlines. Whilst it is not difficult to keep the airlines flying with very high load factors over the summer season, capacity has to be carefully managed so that aircraft capacity is not underutilised during the winter.

Managerial responses:

- Owing to the severity of climatic conditions the Canadian outbound market has a very strong winter demand, particularly to the Caribbean. In 1994 First Choice purchased International Travel Holdings now known as 'Signature Vacations', a Canadian tour operator which carries about 700 000 passengers a year.

- Charter airlines owned by UK tour operators (including Air 2000 owned by First Choice) have developed long-haul routes. On these routes market demand is strongest during the European winter period.

Ease of entry/exit

In some areas of travel and tourism it is relatively easy to set up in business or to leave the business, *i.e.* entry and exist costs are relatively low (compared to some other industries which have higher capital set-up costs). For a tour operator for example, most of the travel services included in the holidays are leased, or are purchased as and when required. The greatest initial cost involved is often in producing the brochures and marketing the holidays to travel agents and the public. Similarly, travel agents do not purchase products from tour operators until the customer pays for them, and so do not incur the risk of unsold stock or stock-holding costs.

Therefore, entry to the industry might be considered to be relatively straightforward and this means that if one company is seen to be successful in a particular segment of the market then it is not difficult for a competitor to offer a similar product.

Interdependence

The travel and tourism industry can be viewed as being comprised of five component sectors:

- accommodation;
- attractions;
- transport;
- travel organisers;
- destination organisations.

Each of these sectors can be further broken down into several sub-divisions (as shown in Fig. 3.1). Some of the sub-divisions, such as tour operators, are operated for profit while others such as museums and national parks are often operated on a non-commercial basis. The important point to note in this context, however, is that the sectors are all linked and depend upon one another, *i.e.* there is an interdependence between them. The accommodation sector, for example, relies upon the transport sector to transport guests to and from the accommodation. Similarly, the transport and accommodation sectors both rely upon the travel organisers sectors to provide them with customers.

If one sector fails to deliver a service it has a 'knock on' effect on other sectors. For example, if a tour operator organizes a holiday including seats on an aircraft, the quality of the holiday will be judged partly upon the quality of the airline regardless of whether the tour operator has any direct control over that airline's activities.

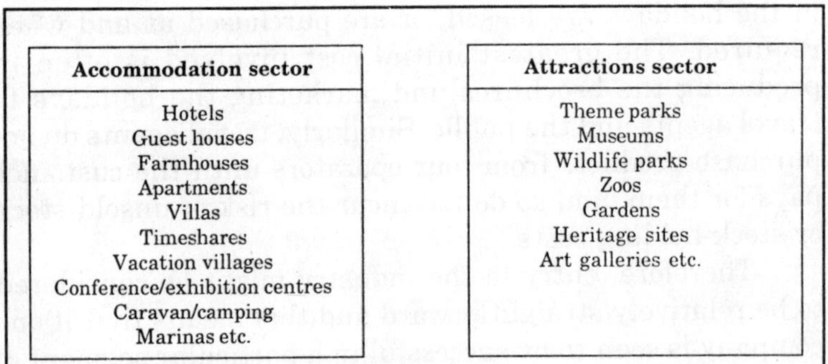

Fig. 3.1— The sectors and sub-divisions of the travel and tourism industry (adapted from Middleton and Clarke, 2001)

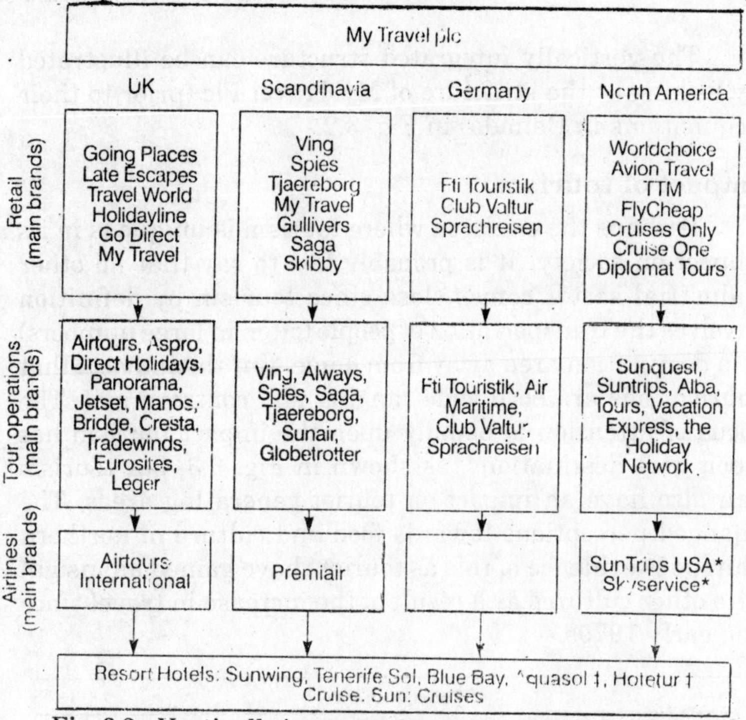

Fig. 3.2—Vertically integrated structure of My Travel plc.
***Long-term contract. Associate. †Joint ventures**
(Airtours plc, 2001)

Figure 3.1 shows how the various sectors in the industry 'fit' together. In reality, the world is not as simple as the diagram suggests. Individual companies will often straddle two or more sectors. Some hotel companies, for example, organise inclusive tour packages and thereby also operate in the travel organisers sector. In the late 1990s travel companies in the UK and elsewhere undertook strategies of 'vertical integration' whereby a single company may sell travel arrangements to customers (retail), provide travel arrangements (tour operations), transport customers (airline operations) and in some cases also own accommodation. As the industry stood in 2002, the 'big 4' outbound travel companies in the UK: Thomson, My Travel (Airtours), First Choice and Thomas Cook, were all vertically integrated in this way.

The vertically integrated structure can be illustrated by looking at the structure of My Travel Plc (prior to their acquisitions in Canada) in Fig. 3.2.

Impact of tourism

Perhaps the one area where tourism is unique is in its impact on society. It is probably fair to say that no other industrial sector comes close since tourism by definition involves the transportation of people (often in large numbers) to a destination area away from home. But the impacts that tourism has are both wide-ranging and controversial. The focus of attention is usually upon the impact tourism has upon host destinations, as shown in Fig. 3.3, but tourism can also have an impact on tourist generating areas. The changed perceptions towards food and culture in northern Europe is evidence of this as tourists have gained an insight into other cultures as a result of the increase in travel since the early 1970s.

Tourist's needs
Travel, Accommodation, Attractions, Shopping, Recreational activity

↓

Tourist industry providers
Cars, Coaches, Road networks, Airlines, Airports, Hotel buildings, Shopping centres, Leisure facilities

↓

Types of impact			
	Economic	***Social***	***Environmental***
Positive impacts	• Visitor spending • Tourism related employment • Investment in infrastructure	• Understanding different cultures • Supporting local services	• Regeneration of urban areas • Preservation of old buildings • Protection of countryside for visitors
Negative impacts	• Leakages of incomce from local economies	• Disturbance of traditional ways of life	• Air, sea and noise pollution Erosion of land-scape and damage to historic buildings

Fig. 3.3—The basic impacts of tourism on destination areas

The holidaymakers

Krippendorf (1987). In his influential work *The Holidaymakers — Understanding the Impacts of Leisure and Travel,* discussed aspects of the impact tourists have on their destination.

'In the early 1960s a leading tourism researcher wrote:

> Tourism brings [people] together, it is instrumental in their dialogue, it leads to personal contact in which people can understand attitudes and beliefs, which were incomprehensible to them, because they were distant. In this way it helps to bridge gaps and erases differences. Since its focal point is man and not the economy, tourism can be one of the most important means, especially in developing countries, of bringing nations closer together and of maintaining good international relations. Hunzikor (1961).
>
> 'This was the theory twenty years ago. Today, when travelling has become a mass phenomenon, the tale of understanding among peoples is nothing more than wishful thinking. Friedrich Wagner (1970), a veteran German travel journalist, argues that the faith in the mission of tourism as promoting international understanding can be supported by a great deal of practical evidence.
>
> 'I do not share this faith nor do I know many positive experiences and examples. On contrary, I believe that the chances for real human contact between holidaymakers and locals could hardly be less hopeful. The contact is usually only skin deep, the relationship a mere illusion. Where the main reason for travelling is to get away from things, where the tourist ignores the existence of other people; where assembly line techniques are the only way of dealing with huge numbers, where profit making rules supreme, where there are feelings of superiority and inferiority, no communication can develop.'

Source: Krippendorf (1987)

Any discussion on the impacts of tourism usually centres on the effects of so-called 'mass-tourism'. Mass tourism has been defined as, 'a phenomenon of large-scale packaging of standardised leisure services at fixed prices for sale to a mass clientele' (Poon, 1993).

Poon went on to identify five key forces as being responsible for the spread of this mass, standardised and rigidly packaged tourism:

1. *Consumers:* sun-lust, and inexperienced mass consumers.
2. *Technology:* jet aircraft, automobile, computer reservations and accounting systems, credit cards.
3. *Production:* cheap oil, charter flights, packaged tours, hotel overbuilding, mass production.
4. *Management:* economies of scale, hotel and holiday branding, promotional airfares, mass marketing.
5. *Frame conditions:* post-war peace and prosperity, paid holidays, regulation of air transportation, incentives to attract hotel chains to establish operations.

In North America and Europe, different agents facilitated the development and spread of mass tourism. In the USA, multinational hotel chains, airlines and the growth in car usage were prevalent whereas in Europe by comparison, powerful tour operators, charter flights and packaged tours to Mediterranean 'sun' destinations, were the key agents in the rapid growth of mass tourism.

One of the key questions facing marketing in a travel and tourism context today is the extent to which mass tourism will continue. Poon (1993), in her book *Tourism, Technology and Competitive Strategies,* claimed that increasingly what she termed as a 'new tourism' is emerging. The signs of the emerging new tourism include:

- The growing demand for 'independent' non packaged holidays.
- The growing demand for choice and flexibility.
- Information technologies, such as Computer Reservations Systems (CRS) and the Internet are rapidly diffusing and allowing customers to deal directly with companies and organisations as a means to flexibly make travel arrangements as an alternative to package holidays.

- The rate of growth of the traditional sun package tour business is slowing.
- There is increasing environmental planning and control of tourism in host countries such as Belize and Bermuda.
- There is an increasing 'segmentation' of travel markets to cater for differing lifestyle characteristics.
- The travel behaviour and motivation of tourists are changing with more shorter breaks and activity oriented travel.

Port Douglas, Queensland, Australia

Tourist destinations and companies are increasingly coming to realise that limits have to be placed on growth if the impacts of tourist developments are not to destroy the attractions that tourists sought in the first place. In the tourism literature the terms 'tourist carrying capacity' and 'sustainable tourism' have been used to describe the maximum desirable level of tourism development that could be sustained over a medium-to long-term period.

Port Douglas is situated about 40 miles north of Cairns on a coast of beautiful beaches, reefs and rainforest. Port Douglas is sharing in the boom of 'Tropical Far North Queensland', the name by which the region markets itself. Once a port handling sugar cane, until 20 years ago it was a sleepy town. Today its permanent population is still only 4000. Port Douglas's resort centre covers only a few streets and traditional wooden buildings surrounded by dense vegetation give the town much of its character. The main 'Four Mile Beach' runs along a strip of land on which Port Douglas is situated. Numerous trips to 'The Great Barrier Reef', 'The Atherton Tablelands' and the 'Daintree Rainforest' world heritage site, also leave the resort.

In 1996 Port Douglas gained a major new hotel with the opening of the 300-room Treetops Resort. It is the latest venture of Port Douglas Reef Resorts and has been designed to the strictest environmental standards and largely leaves the rainforest canopy and tropical foliage intact. The developer also owns the Reef Terraces Resort while Radisson has developed the Radisson Royal Palms Resort close to Four-Mile Beach. Nearby is the Sheraton Mirage Resort while two smaller hotels are located in the centre of the town.

John Morris, Chief Executive of Port Douglas Reef Resorts, has had a big influence on the development of the resort: 'Port Douglas is one of the unique resorts in the world, not just because of its natural attractions but because it will not be changing in any major way. We have about 2000 beds and only a couple more hotels will be allowed. Visitors can rest assured that there will never be a glitzy resort here. It will never go over the top'.

The relevance of the preceding discussion on the impacts of tourism to managers is two fold:

1. Modern consumers are becoming sensitive to the impacts of what they consume, whether it is the effect that the detergents they use might have on the environment or the impacts that tourism has particularly on the host community. In successfully managing their tourism products, managers and marketeers must be sensitive to this issue in a way in which they often were not in the past.
2. Whilst mass tourism may be here to stay, changes are nevertheless taking place in the marketplace. Consumers are becoming more knowledgeable, experienced and sophisticated in their tastes and rather more complicated to understand. Managers have to research and attempt to understand these changes. Furthermore, in the highly competitive travel and tourism industry, they have to design their products to appeal to these changing tastes and then to promote, distribute and price the products appropriately.

The effect of external shocks

The travel and tourism industry is particularly prone to external shocks beyond the control of its managers.

Wars, hurricanes, terrorist attacks, pollution, adverse publicity or accidents can have a dramatic and speedy affect upon levels of business. For example 'The 1990-91 Gulf War' led to a severe downturn in travel and tourism in the early 1990s, whilst the terrorist attacks in New York and Washington on 11 September 2001 had a similar effect upon the industry. Managers, whilst not able to plan directly for such events, need to be able to assess the risks that the business is prone to and have contingency plans in place so that they are able to react quickly and effectively when necessary. One approach is to spread the risks so that one upset does not destroy the business entirely. Thus a tour operator specialising in tours to only country would be vulnerable if a war or environmental catastrophe were to occur in that country. By operating to several countries, however, the risks are spread and the overall vulnerability is reduced.

The effects of September 11 on Accor

Accor is a Paris based multi-brand network of 3600 hotels in 90 countries which are fully integrated in terms of sales and technology. For several years this network has been coordinated under the well known banner of 'Accor Hotels'. Hotel development is based on well-known international brands (such as Sofitel, Novotel, Mercure, Ibis, Formule 1, as well as Motel 6 and Red Roof Inns in the United States), which cover the full range of hotel segments, from budget to luxury class. Accor properties are now well represented around the globe, particularly in America, Europe and Asia.

The travel industry, faced with a slowdown that was already perceptible in the spring of 2001, had to cope with one of the worst crises in its history with the events of September 11 of the same year. The tragic events had two consequences. The first was immediate and of an unprecedented magnitude—a psychological shock. The second was the aggravation of the global economic slowdown affecting America, Europe and Asia simultaneously. As a result of the events, some hotel investments were postponed but very few were cancelled and the group still planned 250 new hotel openings in the early to middle years of the decade. The group was protected to some extent from the worst effects of the downturn by the diversity of its hotel portfolio both geographically and in terms of quality. However, some effects on hotel bookings were inevitable. For example, the luxury hotel industry in Paris was severely affected, whereas the economy hotel segment in Europe held up well. Thus, Sofitel's bookings dropped by 33% in October and 18% in November 2001, while Formule 1 and Ibis budget brands in Europe recorded an increase of 3.5% in their October bookings and 4.6 in November. In the US, Sofitel's bookings declined by 25-30%, whereas Red Roof Inns and Motel 6 (budget brands) registered a limited drop of 8.2% in October and then 6% in November 2001.

4

The Travel and Tourism Organisation—Competencies, Resources and Competitive Advantage

Introduction

We encountered the concept of competitive advantage as one of the key objectives of business strategy. There has been considerable debate in the academic literature as to the causes of competitive advantage. Essentially, the debate asks the question, 'How do organisations achieve superior performance?' Two positions have emerged as the most prominent.

The *competitive positioning* school of thought, based primarily on the work of Professor Michael Porter of Harvard Business School (1980, 1985), stresses the importance of how the organisation is positioned in respect to its competitive environment or industry. The *resource or competence school* (Prahalad and Hamel, 1990; Heene and Sanchez, 1997), on the other hand, argues that it is the competences (abilities) of the business and the distinctive way that it organises, its activities, which determines the ability to outperform competitors. As with most controversies, we suggest that both schools of thought have their merits—both are partial explanations of the source of competitive advantage.

This chapter concentrates on developing an understanding of the major factors governing the level of performance of the business, namely its resources, competences, particularly its core competences, and its 'value adding' activities.

Learning Objectives

After studying this chapter students should be able to:

- explain the concepts of *core competences, competences, resources* and the relationships between them;
- explain the concept of the *value chain* and the value chain framework;
- explain the relationships between core competences and core activities;
- explain how the value chain framework 'works';
- explain how the configuration of value adding activities can improve business performance;
- identify the potential benefits of collaboration with suppliers, distributors and customers.

Resources, competences, core competences and competitive advantage

In all industries, regardless of whether the average profitability for the sector is relatively high or low, some organisations are more successful than others. This is as true for the component sectors of travel and tourism as for any other industry. The superior performers conceivably possess something special that weaker competitors do not have and this enables them to outperform their rivals. The sources of *competitive advantage* lie in combining the superior application of competences (skills) and the deployment of superior resources (assets) in creating value for consumers. Strategy and tourism texts often use the term *sustainable* (or sustainability) in connection with the notion of advantage. Sustainability is achieved when the advantage resists erosion by competitive behaviour (Porter, 1985: 20). In other words, in order to achieve the goal of reaching a position of sustainable competitive advantage, a business's competitive advantage must be capable of resisting duplication or emulation by other companies (Barney, 2002).

Definitions

The terms *competence* and *capability, core competence* and *distinctive capability* are often used interchangeably in textbooks on strategy. Although some writers (Stalk *et al.,* 1992) argued that there are significant differences between the terms *competence* and *capability,* here the terms will be taken to mean broadly the same things based upon the following definitions.

Competences

A *competence* is an attribute or collection of attributes possessed by all or most of the organisations in a sector of industry. Without such attributes a business cannot enter or survive in the industry. Competences develop from resources and embody skills, technology or 'know how'. For example, in order to operate as an outbound tour operator involved in air inclusive tours a company must possess a range of competences in arranging:

- a means of distributing, marketing and selling the product;
- licences to operate the required capacity to the specified destinations;
- air transportation to and from the destination;
- suitable accommodation at the destination;
- ground handling activities to ensure customers are checked on to their flights and that they are transported to and from their accommodation.

Every successful survivor in the industry must possess these areas of competence.

Core competences

A *core competence* or *distinctive capability* is an attribute, or collection of attributes, specific to a particular organisation, which enables it to produce performance above the average for the industry. It arises from the way in which the organisation has employed its competences and resources more effectively than its competitors. The result of a distinctive capability is an output which customers value more highly than those of competitors. The basis upon which their core competences are achieved is considered later in the chapter.

Resources

A *resource* is an input employed in the activities of the business. Success rests in large part upon the efficiency by which the business converts its resources into outputs. Resources fall into five broad categories—human, financial, physical (buildings, equipment, stock, etc.), operational (aeroplanes, ships, coaches etc.) and intangible (*e.g.* 'know how', patents, legal rights, brand names, registered designs, etc.).

Key concept: Competitive advantage

Competitive advantage is often seen as the overall purpose of strategy. Some texts use the phrase *superior performance* to mean the same thing. Essentially, a business can be said to possess competitive advantage if it is able to return higher profits as a proportion of sales than its competitors. The higher profits mean that it will be able to commit more retained profit to reinvestment in its strategy, thus maintaining its lead over its competitors in an industry. When this superiority is maintained successfully over time, a *sustainable* competitive advantage has been achieved. Competitive advantage can be lost when management fail to reinvest the superior profits in such a way that the advantage is not maintained.

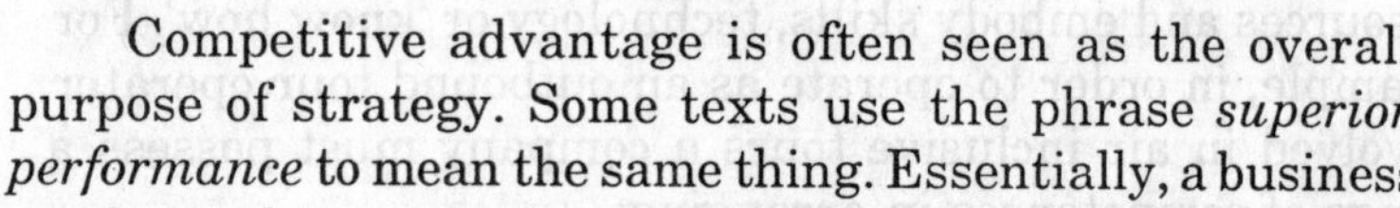

Fig. 4.1—The links between resources, competences and competitive advantage

How core competences 'work'

Core competences tend to be both complex and intangible so that it is necessary to explore the nature of resources and competences which underpin them before exploring the concept further. The purpose of such analysis is to allow managers to identify which resources and competences act as the foundation of existing or potential core competences. It is important to note that not all the competitors in an industry will possess core competences or distinctive capabilities (Kay, 1993). It is only those organisations that are producing above average performance which can be considered as possessing core competences. Those with only average or below average performance possess competences and resources (without which they could not compete in the industry at all) but not core competences. See Prahalad and Hamel (1990), Kay (1993), Heene and Sanchez (1997) and Petts (1997) for further discussion of these concepts.

Made simple

Core competence (distinctive capability) = superior deployment of resources + superior application of 'general' competences.

Core competence (distinctive capability) when applied in a market creates value for customers and this represents competitive advantage

These terms will now be considered in greater detail.

Resource analysis

Tangible and intangible resources

Resources can be either *tangible* or *intangible*. They are the inputs or assets which enable an organisation to carry out its activities. Tangible assets include stocks, materials machinery, buildings, human resources, finance and so on. Intangible assets include skills, knowledge, brand names and goodwill, patent rights, etc. (see Coyne, 1986; Hall 1992), but in a tourism context they also refer to what economists typically refer to as 'free resources'.

Tangible resources are obtained from outside organisations. Such resources are obtained in resource markets in competition with organisations from within and outside the industry. Intangible resources can often be developed within an organisation, but as with tangible resources, they have a value attached to them which, although sometimes difficult to quantify, can often be bought and sold in markets. Relationships with the suppliers of resources can form an important part of the organisation's core competence, as for example with its ability to attract the most appropriately skilled human resources in the job market.

Tourism is different from most other industries in that free resources are a vital part of the product. Free resources are those resources available in such abundance naturally, such as air, the sea, climate and culture, etc., that there is no need for an allocative mechanism (a market), in order to allocate them to users or consumers. Scarce resources on the other hand are the tangible and intangible resources, which are limited in their supply relative to the demand of consumers, and are therefore allocated in a market.

Bull (1995) argued that the basis for tourism lies in building upon free resources (or 'renewable resources' as they are sometimes termed), with a mixture of public sector and private sector resources. Free resources together with the scarce resources are combined to form what most tourists perceive as the tourist 'product'. It may be argued, as Bull (1995) pointed out, that in today's world there are few truly free resources since any human activity makes demands on the world's resources and, as a consequence, ultimately someone will have to pay a price. Indeed the concept of *sustainable tourism* largely rests upon the recognition of such a line of argument.

All resources have competing demands made upon them so that if they are used for one form of activity they cannot be used in other ways. For example, a large flat coastal area might be suitable for the development of a resort area for tourism or as a site for heavy industry. If tourism is chosen ahead of heavy industry an opportunity to develop heavy industry on this site has been lost. The cost of this choice is known as the *opportunity cost,* which represents the potential economic returns that are being given up in favour of the chosen option (in this example, developing tourism).

Features of tourism resources

A number of points are pertinent to a consideration of tourism's use of resources and to their management in the industry. Particular challenges presented to tourism managers in the use of resources include the following.

Resource immobility

Many resources that are used cannot be moved either in terms of place or time. For example, a particular beach or mountain, the Empire State Building or the culture of Spain are geographically fixed. The Alpine shows of February cannot be replicated in May and the 'midnight sun', a tourist attraction in far northern latitudes, can be observed only during midsummer.

Resource substitution

It is often difficult to substitute one resource category with those of another. For example, in a car factory efficiency gains may be possible, and indeed have been achieved, through replacing employees by machines, *i.e.* the substitution of human resources with operational resources. In the case of a luxury hotel, an airline or a cruise ship, for instance, the quality of service is often perceived as being closely linked with the quality and number of staff. Consequently it is difficult to replace human resources with operational resources such as computers, and as a result tourism is usually viewed as a labour intensive industry.

Resource conflict and competition

Tourism frequently makes extensive demands on the use of certain resource, which can be in serious conflict or competition with other uses. Such resource conflict or competition may be partially resolved through pricing mechanisms by which the activity that is able to pay the most is able to use the resources. Similarly, regulatory restrictions such as the geographical zoning of areas to permit specified activities only within a particular zone may resolve some conflicts. Some degree of conflict frequently remains. Thus the competing demands of the British army in using gunnery ranges in the Isle of Purbeck, Dorset (an Area of Outstanding Natural Beauty) and in the Northumberland National Park at Otterburn, Northumberland, are in conflict with tourist demands for unspoilt environments. In a local government setting, tourism has to compete for funding with other activities such as education and social services.

Resource ownership and control

Tourism frequently has to utilise resources that are neither owned nor controlled by the companies operating within the sector. This results in a high degree of interdependence between tourism based business.

Thus airlines depend upon the physical resources provided by airports and the operating resources provided by air traffic control services. Although the airlines may have some influence over the way in which these resources are managed, they are rarely directly owned and managed. Projects aimed at regenerating decaying urban environments often have tourism at their heart. Such projects are often developed as public-private partnerships in which the public sector (local and national government) manage and control the overall redevelopment and provide limited funding (often termed 'pump, priming'). Private sector companies in such cases provide the major part of the financial resources. Examples of such public-private partnerships include the redevelopment of Cardiff Bay in the UK and of the Baltimore waterfront in the USA.

Seasonality

Demand for most tourism resources and hence products, whether business or leisure based, is highly seasonal. This in turn is the result of factors such as climate, the distribution of holiday entitlements, the timing of events and festivals, and historic travel patterns. Consequently, the price that organisations have to pay for their resource inputs and the prices that consumers have to pay those organisations vary according to the season. For example long haul airline flights frequently have a low season, a high season and a 'shoulder' season with prices that reflect periods of relatively high, low and medium levels of demand respectively.

Low rewards

Tourism is often viewed as a low margin area of business. Whilst this is not necessarily the case, it is certainly true to say that the rewards from tourism are often slow to materialise and are susceptible to wide swings in cash flow and profitability. As Bull (1995) pointed out, rewards in tourism may be low for several reasons. The industry is often perceived as being relatively clean and pleasant both to invest in and to work in. Consequently, employees may be prepared to work for lower wages as they would rather work in such an attractive industry than elsewhere. Destinations are often situated in areas with few alternative land uses and employment opportunities and therefore little competition is provided for the use of resources. This puts an effective upper limit on rewards in terms of prices paid for land and development, and wages paid to employees. For example the development of tourism in the Yucatan Peninsula on the Caribbean coast of Mexico, has taken place over recent years in an area that is economically poorly developed and which is remote from major markets for goods and services. Hence the development of tourism in this beautiful region does not face strong competition from other industries for the use of resources and the costs of rewarding resources (in terms of land costs and wages) are relatively low.

Capacity constraints

The capacity of tourism resources is frequently constrained in some way. Thus in tourism the *carrying capacity* for a destination is often referred to. This refers to the ability of a site, resort, or a region to absorb tourism use without deteriorating. The notion of carrying capacity is central to the concept of sustainability. The rapid development of Spain's Costa del Sol for instance from the 1950s onwards demonstrates the need to constrain development. Extensive linear development along the coast to the west of Malaga led to overbuilding with poor planning controls. The relative popularity of the resort area subsequently diminished as consumers opted for more recent and better-planned resorts elsewhere. Thus the over use of resources led to the carrying capacity being exceeded and deterioration in the environment that had attracted tourists in the first place.

Similarly the capacity of physical and operational resources in tourism is often constrained, at least in the short to medium period. If a hotel (physical resource) is full or an airline flight (operational resource) is fully booked it is difficult to add capacity quickly whereas if additional demand is apparent for a manufactured product capacity can often be increased by overtime working, by putting on an extra shift of work or by running production lines at a faster rate. Thus in the tourism industry supply is often relatively fixed whereas demand fluctuates.

The managerial implication of this is that managers will often (in the short to medium term) try to influence demand rather than supply. Thus pricing measures and promotional activities will be altered in order to increase or reduce demand so that it matches the supply that is available. For example it has become common for UK tour operators to alter prices in a very active manner in the weeks immediately prior to the date of departure and hotels often make late alterations to their accommodation rates. This active management of prices (which can be moved upwards or downwards to inhibit or encourage demand respectively) is a way of managing the demand so that it matches the supply which has been previously fixed.

Time

Unlike the purchase of household goods or many services, tourism consumers must also give up a scarce resource in addition to money, namely time. In a similar way to money, time has an 'opportunity cost' attached to it, *i.e.* other ways in which it might be spent to which a value can be attached. Whilst much time is spent on tourism willingly, other time spent travelling may be viewed by some consumers as a burden that if at all possible should be avoided or curtailed. The managerial implication of this is that consumers may choose different products or may be willing to pay a premium for certain services or alternatively take advantage of discounted travel in return for some extra inconvenience.

For example, flights to Australia from Europe have become increasingly popular for leisure travellers in recent years as newer aircraft types (primarily the Boeing 747 400 series) have needed only one refuelling stop, thereby reducing journey times to about 21 hours. The more efficient use of time also explains why overnight long haul flights and early morning trains are more expensive. The recent rapid growth in the popularity of 'no-frills' airlines is explained partly by the fact that passengers are willing to trade some degree of inconvenience for lower fares. The airlines usually utilise 'secondary airports' (such as London Luton airport in the UK or Dallas Love Field in the USA) which are further away from the main urban centres that they serve.

Analysing resources

When we analyse a company's resources as part of an internal analysis, several frameworks can be employed to provide a comprehensive review.

Analysis by category

First, we might consider them by *category*—physical, operational, human, financial and intangible resources. These resources are then evaluated quantitatively (how much or how many) and qualitatively (how effectively they are being employed). Much of this analysis is covered in Chapters 4, 5 and 6.

- Physical resources (buildings, land, materials) and operational resources (computers, machines, aircraft, systems etc.) are typically be audited for capacity, utilisation, age, condition, contribution to output and value.
- Financial resources (the amount and type of finance available to the organisation) are considered in terms of the balance between different types of finance and the relative cost of the each of these types.
- Human resources (employees, junior, middle and senior management, board directors) are considered in terms of numbers, education, skills, training, experience, age, motivation, wage costs and productivity in relation to the needs of the organisation.
- Intangible resources (brand, reputation, goodwill, skills and 'free' resources) are assessed in terms of their overall value to the organisation.

Resource analysis for Marriott International

Marriott International is a leading worldwide hospitality company which operates and franchises hotels under a number of recognised international brand names including Marriott, Renaissance and Ramada International.

Resource category	Analysis of Marriott resources
Physical resources	• Over 2200 operating units in the United States and 59 other countries. • Properties range from luxurious (Ritz-Carlton) to budget (Courtyard and Fairfield Inn).

Operational resources	• Each brand has a detailed set of operating procedures which is constantly updated and refined. • Worldwide reservations system with industry leading costs per reservation. • Common reservations system for all brands allowing for cross selling opportunities. • Large web sales volume. • Marriott Rewards is the largest frequent guest programme in the hospitality sector and is linked to over 30 international airlines.
Financial resources	• Most hotels are financed by third parties with only 1% of properties being company-owned. • As a hotel manager and franchiser significant and more stable cash flows are generated than through real estate ownership. • Strong balance sheet and profitability record.
Human resources	• 153 000 employees. • Extensive staff training and advancement opportunities. • Largest employer in 'Fortune' list of 100 best companies to work for in United States.
Intangible resources	• Strong range of brand names many of which are clear leaders within their market tiers. • Customer and owner loyalty achieved through a strong rewards programme • Distinct market positioning of each brand. • Many hotels situated at scenic locations.

Analysis by specificity

Secondly, we can analyse resources according to their *specificity.* Resources can be specific or non-specific. For example, skilled workers tend to have specialised and industry-specific knowledge and skills. Some technology, for example computer software, is for general (non industry-specific) business use, like word-processing, database and spreadsheet software. Other computer software applications, like airline or hotel computer reservation systems, or yield management programme, are written for highly specialised uses. Whereas non-specific resources tend to be more flexible and form and basis of competences, industry-specific resources are more likely to act as the foundations of core competences (for example the specialised knowledge of procurement managers responsible for contracting accommodation in the tour operating sector).

Analysis by performance

Thirdly, resources can be evaluated on the basis of how they contribute to internal and external *measures of performance.* Internal measures include their contribution to:

- business objectives and targets—financial performance and output measures;
- historical comparisons—measures of performance over time (*e.g.* against previous years);
- business unit or divisional comparisons.

External measures can include:

- comparisons with competitors, particularly those who are industry leaders and those who are the closest competitors and are in its strategic grouping;
- comparisons with companies in other service based industries.

By employing these techniques of analysis, an organisation is able to internally and externally *benchmark* its performance as a stimulus to improving performance in the future. Performance, however, is based on more than resources, and competences must be similarly analysed and evaluated.

Competences

Competences are attributes like skills, knowledge, technology and relationships that are common among the competitors in an industry. For example, all companies in the airline industry possess similar competences (basic abilities) in operations, marketing and distribution. They are less tangible than resources and are consequently more difficult to evaluate. Competences are more often developed internally but may also be acquired externally or by collaboration with suppliers, distributors or customers.

Competences are distinguished from core competences by the fact that they do not produce superior performance and by the fact that they are not distinctive when compared to the competences possessed by other companies in the industry. On the other hand, competences are essential for survival in a particular line of business. Competences also have the potential to be developed into core competences.

Core competences

Distinguishing core competences from general competences

Core competences are distinguished from competences in several ways:

- they are only possessed by those companies whose performance is superior to the industry average;
- they are unique to the company;
- they are more complex;
- they are difficult to emulate (copy);
- they relate to fulfilling customer needs;
- they add greater value than 'general' competences;
- they are often based on distinctive relationships with customers, distributors and suppliers;
- they are based upon superior organisational skills and knowledge.

Core competence arises from the unique and distinctive way that the organisation builds, develops, integrates and deploys its resources and competences. An existing core competence can be evaluated for:

- *Customer focus*—does it adequately focus on customer needs?
- *Uniqueness*—can it be imitated by competitors as if so, how easily?
- *Flexibility*—can it be easily adapted if market or industry conditions change?
- *Contribution to value*—to what extent does it add value to the product or service?
- *Sustainability*—how long can its superiority be sustained over time?

Competences, as opposed to core competences, can also be judged against these criteria in order to evaluate their potential to form the basis upon which new core competences can be built.

Core competences can never be regarded as being permanent. The pace of change of technology and society are such that core competences must be constantly adapted and new ones cultivated.

Sustaining core competences—Club Med

In 1950, with Europe at peace, Frenchman Gillbert Trigano together with Gerard Blitz, a Belgian, bought some American army surplus tents and camp beds, set them up in a pinewood on the Spanish island of Majorca and called the enterprise Club Mediterranee. The idea was a success from the start. Holiday camps were not new. In Britain Billy Butlin's camps had provided cheap refuges from rainy summers. But Club Med (as it became known) offered reliable sunshine and warm seas, along with what Gerard Blitz called 'an antidote to civilisation'. He saw no need for Club Med to make money, as long as they covered their costs. What mattered was that people could be liberated from their working lives for a week or two and live as the noble savage, do some cooking if they wanted to and help with the rudimentary washing-up. It was Trigano who turned Club Med into a profitable business. Tents were soon replaced by thatched huts. During Mr. Trigano's four decades with Club Med, bungalows and hotels were added with the soft comforts of home. Staff were hired to do the chores. There were Club Med establishments throughout the world from Tahiti to Bulgaria.

The romanticism that had made Club Med so appealing when Trigano and his early partner banged in the first tent pegs in Majorca was not discarded. Rather, Trigano made Club Med's hint of sensual pleasure a key part of its sales appeal. The partly Belgian idea, which had been launched in Spain with American equipment, became as French as Bardot. As a loyal Frenchman, Mr. Trigano made Club Med a messenger of his country's superiority in food, wine, language and indeed culture. Then, suddenly, it seemed that paradise was lost.

After Club Med had showed losses for three successive years in the 1990s, Harvard Business School chillingly used the firm as a study to illustrate 'the death of a brand'. Club Med, which a survey revealed that 77% of Americans and 88% of Europeans had heard of, had become Club Red. The young people who were once its customers were now middle-aged and less thrilled by its offer of organised, communal living, however comfortable. The next generation saw Club Med as just another big hotel chain.

After a revolt by shareholders of Club Med in 1997 Mr. Trigano and his son Serge, who had become chief executive, stood down from management. Philippe Bourgignon, who had revived Disney's sickly theme park near Paris, took over, with a promise to return Club Med back to health. Over the next three years the Group transformed its activities and staged a strong financial recovery. After being tested in the French market in 1998, the new group strategy was put into practice in 1999. Restoring the brand and distribution, regaining competitiveness and rationalizing management and organisation all contributed to strengthening the Club's market position.

The Club now enjoys an improved image, better product—client fit, a fair price policy, rising volumes and profitable product delivery. A new leisure concept Club Med World (a city based product) was successfully launched, the Club Med product range was broadened to include active wear, body care and sun creams, sunglasses, watches, water sports, etc. and Club Med.com was developed as a new distribution channel. With its transformation plan, strong growth has been achieved utilizing its three strategic assets: its employees, its members and its brand (a 'club'). In so doing the company is repositioning itself from being a hotel company to a service company based on the concept of a 'club' and on the strong sense of belonging which its members (750 000 in France alone) enjoy, enabling it to embody a lifestyle.

Core competences and distinctive capabilities

Kay (1993) presented a slightly different explanation arguing that competitive advantage is based upon what he termed *distinctive capability*. According to Kay (1993), distinctive capability can develop from four sources:

- *Architecture*—A network of relationships within or around the organisation. The relationships may be among employees (internal architecture), with suppliers and customers (external architecture) or among a group of organisations engaged in related activities (networks). For example, the strategic alliances that have been built up by the major international airlines in recent years are examples of using networks to strengthen the competitive position of individual airlines through shared activities and extending geographical scope.
- *Reputation*—In service markets reputation is an extremely important contributor to consumer choice of product, but given the intangibility of the product, reputation is usually built up slowly and at some cost as consumers gain experience. Given the high value and public profile of travel products,

reputations can easily be damaged, for example, through disaster. A coach or aeroplane crash, a ferry sinking or a hotel fire quickly erodes the reputation of the affected organisation.

- *Strategic assets*—The strength of market position or dominance of a market is often based upon the possession of strategic assets. They can be of three types. First, an organisation may benefit from a monopoly position in a market, secondly, an organisation may have already incurred the costs of supplying a market which inhibits the ability of new entrants to compete effectively, and thirdly, some companies may benefit from the possession of licences or regulation that prevents competition. For example, the dominant position of major international airlines at their 'hub' airports (such as Lufthansa at Frankfurt, United at Chicago and American Airlines at Dallas/Fort Worth) is often the result of costs expended over many years and local regulatory regimes that have allocated take-off and landing slots to these airlines over the years.
- *Innovation*—Through innovation companies are often capable of providing a distinctive product and/or reducing costs. However, innovations can often be copied (particularly in service industries) and the additional returns are often not forthcoming for the innovating company. For example, British Airways was the world's first airline to introduce flat beds for some of its business class passengers, but other airlines quickly followed its lead.

British Airways' core competences

In the airline sector all airlines have the competences and resources required to operate flights between certain destinations. A company like British Airways (Kay, 1993) possesses core competences relating to its:

- Dominance of take off and landing slots at London's Heathrow airport.

- Licences it holds to operate certain routes to which access is denied for other airlines.
- Brand attributes which act as the basis of its reputation for high quality for other airlines.

These core competences, although initially identified by the author in the early 1990s, are still valid in the contemporary market. However, it could be argued that the web of cooperative partnerships with other airlines through the 'One World' strategic alliance in allowing for greater destination choice and flexibility of arrangements provides a further area of core competence for the airline. Thus British Airways has distinctive capabilities in terms of strategic assets (Heathrow slots and licences), reputation (brand attributes) and architecture (strategic alliances).

The possession of these core competences enables the airline to charge premium prices for its products by targeting business travellers in particular and by altering aircraft seat configurations to accommodate a greater proportion of business and first class passengers. In this way, core competences are applied to the marketplace and in so doing form the basis of an organisation's competitive advantage.

Outcomes of the analysis

Aims of the analysis

The aims of an analysis of resources, competences and core competences (distinctive capabilities) are, therefore, to:

- understand the nature and sources of particular core competences;
- identify the need for and methods of adaptation of existing core competences;
- identify the need for new core competence building;
- identify potential sources of core competence based on resources and competences;
- ensure that core competences remain focused on customer needs.

Resources, competences and core competences are obviously closely related to the ways that a business organises and performs its value adding activities. It is therefore also necessary to analyse the way in which value adding activities are configured and co-ordinated.

Competence leveraging and building

Competence leveraging

Competence leveraging refers to the ability of a business to exploit its core competences in new markets, thus meeting new customer needs. It can also refer to the ability of the business to modify and improve existing core competences.

Competence building

Competence building takes place when the business builds new core competences, based upon its resources and competences. It is often necessary to build new competences alongside existing ones when entering new markets as it is unlikely that existing competences will fully meet new customer needs.

From distinctive capability to competitive advantage

According to Kay (1993), distinctive capability becomes a competitive advantage when it is applied in a relevant market. Each distinctive capability will have a market (or group of markets) in which the organisation can achieve a competitive advantage. Competitive advantage is a relative rather than an absolute notion and can be viewed in several ways.

Organisations can enjoy a competitive advantage relative to:

- other suppliers in the same market;
- other firms in the same industry; or,
- other competitors in the same strategic grouping.

In establishing competitive advantage therefore, it is important that activities are correctly matched up to the organisation's capabilities. It is also important that organisations are able to fully understand the inherent differences between: 'the market', 'the industry' and the 'strategic group'. The market refers to the needs of customers and potential customers, whereas the industry an organisation is in refers to a group of products linked by common technology, supply or distribution channels. The strategic group refers to those organisations that are identified as primary competitors.

Markets, industries and strategic groups

The market

- Defined by demand conditions;
- Based on consumer needs;
- Characterised by 'the law of one price'.

The industry

- Determined by supply conditions;
- Based on production or operations technology;
- Defined by the markets chosen by organisations.

The strategic group

- Defined by the strategic choices of firms;
- Based on distinctive capabilities and market positioning;
- Subjective in determination.

During the 1980s Britain's largest brewer, Bass plc, viewed the market for beer as having unexciting growth prospects and redefined its core business as 'leisure'. Consequently the company bought Horizon Travel, a leading UK tour operator of the time. Bass was correct in its observation that pubs and holidays were alternative ways of spending leisure time and that they competed for the same share of consumer expenditure. However, the skills involved in brewing beer and managing an estate of public houses were quite different from those required to run a tour operator. As a result, the tour operator was subsequently disposed of through a sale to the market leader, Thomson. Bass, perhaps failed fully to appreciate that there is a leisure market but that there is not a leisure industry. They did not possess the necessary operating skills (in the industry) to service the market effectively.

Source: Adapted from Kay (1993)

Analysis of value adding activities

What is value adding?

Value chain analysis (Porter, 1985) seeks to provide an understanding of how much value an organisation's activities add to its products and services compared to the costs of the resources used in their production. Although it has been applied widely in the manufacturing sector, several writers have applied the model successfully to a service setting. Poon (1993), for example, adapted the model to the travel and tourism industry. A given product can be produced by organising activities in a number of different ways. Value chain analysis helps managers to understand how effectively and efficiently the activities of their organisation are configured and coordinated. The acid test is how much value is added in the process of turning inputs into the outputs, which are products in the form of goods and services. Value is measured in terms of the price that customers are willing to pay for the product.

Value added can be increased in two ways. It can be increased by:

1. changing customer perceptions of the product so that they are willing to pay a higher price for a product than for similar products produced by other businesses; or by,
2. reducing unit costs of production below those of competitors.

Key concept: value added

In simple terms, the value added to a good or service is the difference in the financial value of the finished product compared to the financial value of the inputs. As a sheet of metal passes through the various stages in car production, value is added so that a tonne of metal worth a few hundred pounds becomes a motor car worth several thousand pounds. The rate at which value is added is dependent upon how well the operations process is managed. If the car manufacturer suffers a cost disadvantage by, say, holding a high level of stock or working with out-of-date machinery, then the value added over the process will be lower.

Similarly, a tour operator gathers together various inputs in terms of transportation, accommodation, on-site services and ground handling arrangements and 'packages' them together and in so doing adds value to the customer. Efficiencies in procurement, for instance, achieved through the use of buying in bulk can be passed on to the customer.

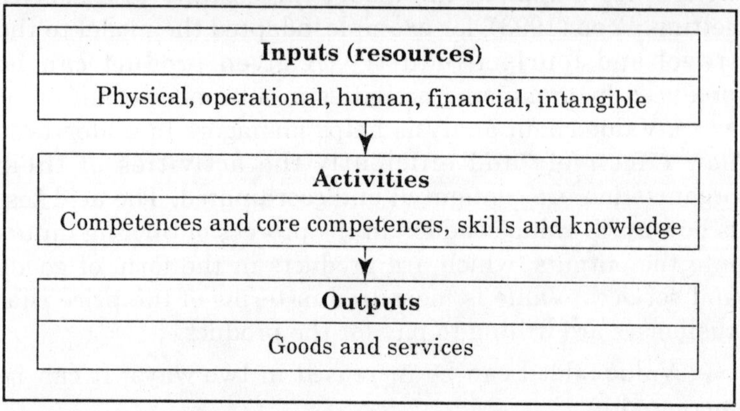

Fig. 4.2—A simplified schematic of the value adding process.

There are clear linkages between value adding activities, core competences, competences and resources. Resources form the inputs to the organisation's value adding activities while competences and core competences provide the skills and knowledge required to carry them out. The more that core competences can be integrated into value adding activities, the greater will be the value added.

The value adding process

Businesses can be regarded as systems that transform inputs (resources, materials, etc.) into outputs (goods and services).

The activities inside the organisation *add value* to the inputs. The value of the products is equivalent to the price that a customer is willing to pay for them. The difference between the end value and the total costs is the *margin* (the quantity that accountants would refer to as the *profit margin*—before interest, taxation and extraordinary items). The rate at which value is added varies. If value is not being added as fast as it could be then *waste* is occurring and the organisation is not operating as efficiently as it might. Poor quality, low utilisation or occupancy and an under-skilled workforce are all examples of waste. Increased added value can be achieved through achieving a reduction in costs or increasing the price that the customer is willing to pay for the output.

The value chain

The activities of the organisation can be broken down into a sequence of activities known as the *value chain* as described by Porter in 1985. Poon (1993) applied Porter's value chain to the travel and tourism industry (See Fig. 4.3).

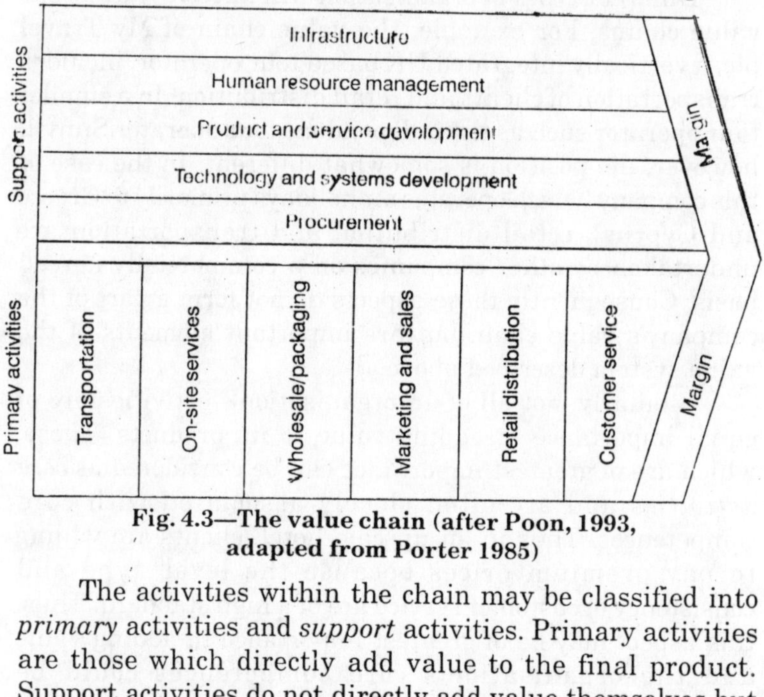

Fig. 4.3—The value chain (after Poon, 1993, adapted from Porter 1985)

The activities within the chain may be classified into *primary* activities and *support* activities. Primary activities are those which directly add value to the final product. Support activities do not directly add value themselves but indirectly add value by supporting the effective execution of primary activities. Whilst the nature of the primary activities and the way in which they can add value vary greatly between differing types of tourism organisation according to the organisational context, the secondary activities are common in most organisational contexts.

Tables 4.1 and 4.2 describe the primary and support relating to the travel and tourism industry and how they might add value.

Analysis of the value chain

An organisation's value chain links into the value chains of other organisations, particularly those of suppliers and distributors. This 'chain' of value chains is sometimes called the *value system* or *total supply chain*. Linkages with suppliers are known as forward linkages while those with distributors and customers are backward linkages.

Different types of organisation will have very different value chains. For example, the value chain of My Travel plc, a vertically integrated UK based tour operator, includes transportation of clients and retail distribution. In a smaller tour operator such as the independent tour operator Sunvil, however, the position is somewhat different. In the case of this company (which operates air holidays primarily to Greece and Cyprus), retail distribution and transportation are undertaken by other companies on a commercially agreed basis. Consequently these aspects do not form a part of the company's value chain but are important elements of the value system described above.

Similarly, not all of an organisation's activities are of equal importance in adding value to its products. Those, which are of greatest importance can be considered as *core activities* and are often closely associated with core competences. Thus in an upscale hotel, clients are willing to pay premium prices because the level, type and consistency of customer service are of a high standard. Thus, this aspect may be of greatest importance in adding value and the organisation's core competences could be concentrated in this area.

Table 4.1—Primary activities (adapted from Poon, 1993.

Activity	Description	Examples of how value might be added
Transportation services	Transportation to and from the destination and at the destination	Information provision Scheduling Gate operations Ticketing Baggage handling Passenger management In flight/on board services Reservations Route and yield management Equipment age and specification Timekeeping
Services on site	Services delivered to visitors at their destination	Repair and maintenance of accommodation Age and specification of accommodation Entertainment Added services provided, *e.g.* car hire, excursions Accommodation locations Quality of company representatives
Wholesaling and packaging	Assembling or 'packaging' the product or service	Commission negotiations Product development Pricing Assembling, integrating and coordinating aspects of the product
Retail distribution	Distributing the product to the market	Retail locations Choice of distribution channels Commission levels Cost of sales Client database management Customer retention levels
Marketing and sales	Making the product available to the market and	Brochure production and distribution Advertising

	persuading people to buy.	Public relations Sales force management Frequent flyer programmes Brochure display Point of sale materials
Customer service	Installation and after sales support	Customer complaint management Management and monitoring customer satisfaction Speed of responsiveness Client advice.

Table 4.2—Support activities (adapted from Poon, 1993)

Activity	Description	Examples of how value might be added
Procurement	Purchasing, leasing or renting of services and equipment	Lower prices Better contract terms
Technology and systems development	Developing and implementing technology and systems in support of primary activities	Computer reservation systems Internet applications 'Real-time' sales reports Yield management applications
Products and Services development	Developing new products, services and market opportunities	New Market segments New products New destinations Developing partnerships and alliances
Human resource management	Recruitment, selection, training, reward and motivation	Quality of employees and managers Employee empowerment Team working Level of training Outsourcing
Infrastructure	General management, financial control and accounting, planning, legal affairs, quality control	Speed and quality of decision making Costs of providing infrastructure Coherent and consistent standards

A further point to stress is the importance of linkages between the component parts of the model. In some cases a key source of value added activity might lie in the way in which organisations link different parts of the value chain. For example for a tour operator it is important that demand and supply are closely coordinated so that excess capacity which cannot be sold is avoided and so that there is enough supply to meet customer demand. This involves close linkages between the transportation, wholesaling and packaging, retail distribution and marketing and sales components.

Analysis of value adding activities helps to identify where the most value is added and where there is potential to add greater value by changing the way in which activities are configured and by improving the way in which they are coordinated. It is important to note that an organisation's value chain is not analysed in isolation but that it is considered in conjunction with its external linkages to suppliers, distributors and customers. Figure 4.3 provides a classification of various internal and external linkages encountered.

A value chain analysis would be expected to include:

- a breakdown of all the activities of the organisations;
- identification of core activities and their relationships to core competences and current organisational strategies;
- identification of the effectiveness and efficiency of the individual activities;
- examination of *linkages* between activities for additional added value;
- identification of *blockages* which reduce the organisation's competitive advantage.

A useful technique in value chain analysis involves comparison with the value chains of competitors to identify the benefits and drawbacks of alternative configurations.

The aim of value chain analysis is to identify ways in which the performance of the individual activities and the linkages between them can be improved. This may involve identification of improved configurations for activities or improved coordination of them. It is particularly important

Table 4.3—Classification of internal and external linkages

Internal linkages		External linkages	
Type of activity	**Example**	**Type of activity**	**Example**
Primary-primary	Interdepartmental coordination	Links with suppliers—backward linkages (upstream)	Tour operator with a hotel group
Primary-support	Computer base sales management systems	Links with distributors—forward linkages (downstream)	Tour operator securing 'racking agreement' with a travel agency group for its brochures.
Support-support	Training for new technologies	Links with other companies at same stage of operations	Airlines collaborating in some of their activities through the formation of strategic alliances

to consider the extent to which value chain activities support the current strategy of the organisation. For example, if the current strategy is based upon high quality then the activities must be configured so as to ensure the creation of high quality products. On the other hand, if the organisation competes largely on the basis of price then activities must be organised so as to minimize costs.

Core activities, non-core activities and outsourcing

An increasing trend in recent years has been for organisations to concentrate on core activities associated with core competences and to outsource activities which are not regarded as core to other organisations for whom those activities are core. This is why, for example, British Airways has outsourced some of its accounting and information technology functions to external suppliers. The combination of complementary core competences adds to the competitive advantage of all the collaborating companies. Value chain analysis should therefore also seek to identify where outsourcing might potentially add greater value than performing the activity in-house.

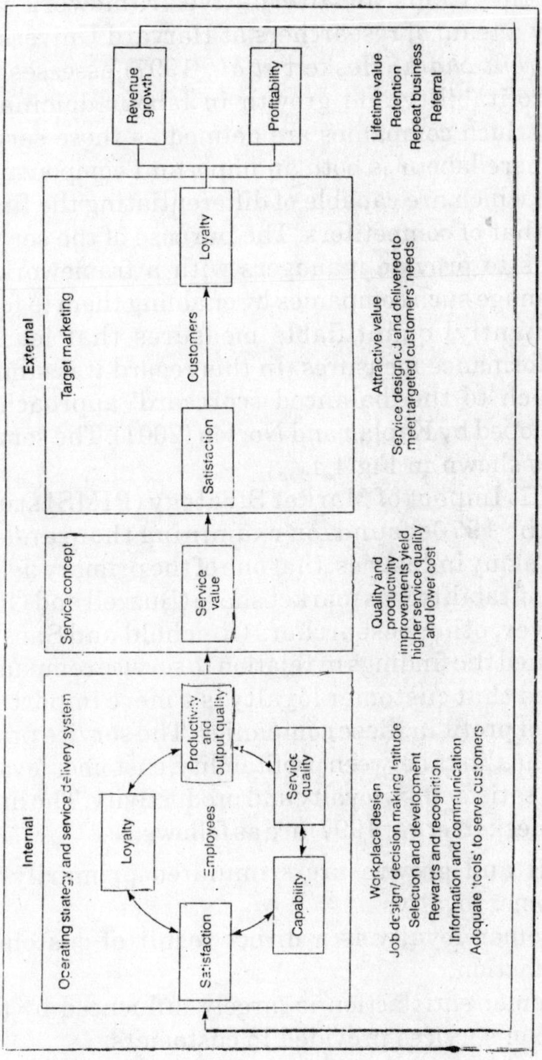

Fig.4.4—The service profit chain (adapted from Heskett et. at., 1997)

The service profit chain

During the 1990s an alternative framework was introduced by a team of researchers at Harvard University. The *service profit chain* (Heskett *et al.*, 1997) assesses the sources of profitability and growth in labour dominated service firms. Such companies are defined as those service companies where labour is both an important component of total cost and which are capable of differentiating the firm's service from that of competitors. The purpose of the service profit chain is to provide managers with a framework to help them manage such companies by enabling them to focus on (predominantly) quantifiable measures that lead to financial performance measures. In this regard it is similar in its approach to the 'balanced scorecard' approach to strategy developed by Kaplan and Norton (2001). The service profit chain is shown in Fig 4.4.

The Profit Impact of Market Strategy (PIMS) study initiated in the 1970s found, on examining thousands of companies in many industries, that one of the primary determinants of profitability was market share (Buzzell and Gale, 1992). However, other researchers (Reicheld and Sasser, 1990) questioned the findings in relation to service companies and concluded that customer loyalty is a more important determinant of profit in these companies. The service profit chain establishes links between profitability, customer loyalty and employee satisfaction, loyalty and productivity. The links in the chain (Heskett *et al.*, 1997) are as follows:

- Profit and growth are stimulated primarily by customer loyalty.
- Customer loyalty is a direct result of customer satisfaction.
- Customer satisfaction is largely influenced by the value of services provided to customers.
- Value is created by satisfied, loyal, and productive employees.
- Employee satisfaction results primarily from high quality support services and policies that enable employees to deliver results to customers.

5

The Travel and Tourism Organisation—The Human Context

Introduction

Human resources are one of the key resource inputs to any organisational process. A thorough analysis of this resource is an important part of strategic analysis and this chapter explains the resource audit—one of the most widely used tools for this purpose.

Closely linked to the human resource is the issue of an organisation's personality or culture. We define culture and then go on to explain its importance to an organisation. The cultural web is discussed—a model used to explain the way that the features of culture determine the organisation's paradigm. Finally, we discuss two cultural typologies.

Learning Objectives

After studying this chapter, students should be able to:

- define and explain the importance of human resources to an organisation;
- explain the employment and working conditions in tourism;
- explain the purpose of a human resource audit;
- describe what a human resource gap is;

- explain what a human resource audit contains and what it can be used for;
- describe human resource benchmarking;
- explain what a critical success factor (CSF) is and how human resources can be CSFs;
- define culture, explain its determinants and why it is important;
- explain the components of the cultural web and the nature of paradigms;
- describe two typologies of cultural types.

Human resources

The importance of human resources

People are an important resource to most organisations, but in service based organisations in particular it is often the human resources (*i.e.* people) that represent the key factor in delivering successful performance. Lynch (2000) put it thus, 'There are some industries where people are not just important but they are the *key factor* for successful performance, as for example in leisure and tourism, where a company has a direct, intangible interface that relies on individual employees to give interest and enjoyment to customers'. Similarly, Baum (1997) considered the experience of the guest or consumer within the tourism industry to be both highly intense and intimate in a way rarely replicated in other service industries. Furthermore, their interactive experience is commonly with the industry's front-line staff who generally are those who have the lowest status, are the least highly trained and are the poorest paid employees. Several authors, including Baum (1995), Choy (1995) and Nickson (2000), have investigated these characteristics.

The importance of employee performance in tourism—Marriott Hotels

Notwithstanding the sales oriented language (designated to attract potential recruits), the following extract from Marriott Hotels clearly illustrates the importance the American based hotel chain attaches to selecting, recruiting and motivating its employees:

> 'Recognising our associates [employees] for their hard work, providing for their health and the well-being of their family members, opening avenues of growth and career development, easing the balance between work and personal life—are all part of our associate-centred environment.
>
> 'At Marriott our success begins with our associates. The idea that highly satisfied associates provide better service to customers is the foundation of our philosophy. It's a great formula: when our associates delight our customers, those customers will return and add to our business. And a successful business means growth and greater opportunities for our associates.
>
> 'As a result you will find a culture that supports and inspires personal development both within the workplace and beyond. Mentoring, training, advancement paths, career mobility, and work-life programmes are just a few of the initiatives and programmes that bring to life our forward-thinking approach toward careers. Marriott's diverse environment readily recognises the contributions of individuals and, at the same time, maximizes the synergy that close teamwork can bring. In addition, we are committed to promoting from within whenever possible.'

Source: Adapted from Marriott.com

Employment and working conditions in travel and tourism

Worldwide employment in tourism is estimated at 192.2 million jobs which is one in every 12.4 jobs. By 2010 this should grow to 251.6 million jobs (one in every 11 jobs) according to the World Travel and Tourism Council (WTTC, 2000). The industry employs a large proportion of young and female employees and has a large number of part-time and seasonal workers. The industry is also often characterised by:

- a large proportion of female employees;
- a large proportion of young employees;

- a large number of part-time and seasonal workers;
- high staff turnover rates;
- recruitment difficulties;
- poor levels of training;
- low pay.

A study in the United States (Woods *et al.*,1998), for example, found that annual staff turnover in the hotel sector was running at 51.7% for 'front-line' employees (although the figures were somewhat lower for supervisory and managerial staff). As a counter-balance to some of the negative aspects of the industry, it must be said that the industry is often seen as an attractive industry in which to work. Staff often have access to concessionary travel and accommodation rates, opportunities are presented for meeting people and seeing something of the world and many employees are situated in attractive surroundings.

In such circumstances the challenge to managers is to recruit and retain well motivated employees. In order to do this employers may offer more training opportunities, provide higher levels of pay and bonuses and pay attention to the design of jobs and roles through:

- *job enlargement*—by which employees' jobs are made more worthwhile and interesting in that they are given a wider variety of tasks to carry out;
- *job rotation*—by which employees rotate jobs between them so that teamwork is encouraged, knowledge and skills are gained and everyone has to take a share of less popular tasks;
- *job enrichment*—by which employees are given a greater deal of discretion or empowerment to make decisions;
- *job sharing*—by which employees' jobs are shared between two or more employees thereby sharing burdens and responsibilities.

The management of the guest—employee encounter

The management of the guest (or customer)-employee encounter remains one of the most difficult but ultimately most important tasks for tourism managers (Baum,1997). Thus, in fast moving markets, especially in service industries which are relatively 'labour intensive', the following factors are particularly important:

- the abilities and knowledge of individuals;
- the ability of individuals to learn;
- the ability of individuals to adapt to change (Pettigrew and Whipp, 1991).

Writers on service quality have suggested that, 'the proof of service [quality] is in its flawless performance' (Berry and Parasuraman, 1991)—a concept similar to the notion of 'zero defects' which is often discussed in a manufacturing context. From the customer's point of view, the most immediate evidence of service quality occurs in the service encounter or 'the moment of truth' when the customer interacts with the organisation (Bitner *et al.*, 1994). The derivation of the term 'moment of truth' is often attributed to Jan Carlzon (1987), a past President of Scandinavian Airline Systems (SAS), when he used the terminology to describe every point of contact that a customer, or potential customer, has with the organisation in question.

As Baum (1995) and Ryan (1996) have argued, the tourism industry presents particular challenges in the management of 'moments of truth' because of the fragmentation of the experience for many customers. For example, the purchase of a typical package holiday may involve contact with a wide range of intermediaries. The following list is indicative only (adapted from Baum,1997). Each one is potentially involved in a 'moment of truth'.

- The retail travel agent;
- Insurance companies;
- Ground transport to and from the airport;
- Airport handling agents (at outbound and inbound airports);
- Immigration and customs services;
- Local ground transportation;
- The hotel or other accommodation;

- Tour services at the destination;
- Companies selling goods and services at the destination;
- Emergency services at the destination;
- Service providers such as photography processing on return.

The concept of the 'moment of truth' as a manifestation of the guest (or customer)—employee encounter clearly has applicability throughout the three parts (traveller generator region, transit route region and tourist destination region) of what Leiper (1990) called 'the tourism system'. Baum, building on Leiper's representation, produced a model of 'moments of truth' in relation to the wide range of organisations that go to make up the tourism system. The model presented as Fig. 5.1 recognises that 'moments of truth' need not carry equal weighting, *i.e.* some will be more important to customers than others, 'so that as far as the guest is concerned... a positive or negative experience in one area may elicit a very different response to a similar experience elsewhere in the guest cycle' (Baum, 1997). The model provides through its vertical axis a measure (albeit rather crude and subjective) of the intensity and therefore the importance of the interaction to customers. In so doing the model allows tourism managers who are responsible for the tourists' experience to attempt to predict those areas of greatest potential impact and consequently to recognise those areas on which resources might be focused.

Decisions about the future strategy of the organisation are made by people and strategies are implemented by people. The success or failure of a current strategy will depend not only on decisions made in the past but also on how those decisions are being implemented now by people employed by the organisation. It is therefore important to ask questions about who and how, and about why people are doing what they are doing and what they should do in strategic implementation. In short, human resources add value, manage the business and, conversely, can make spectacular errors that can be very costly to the organisation.

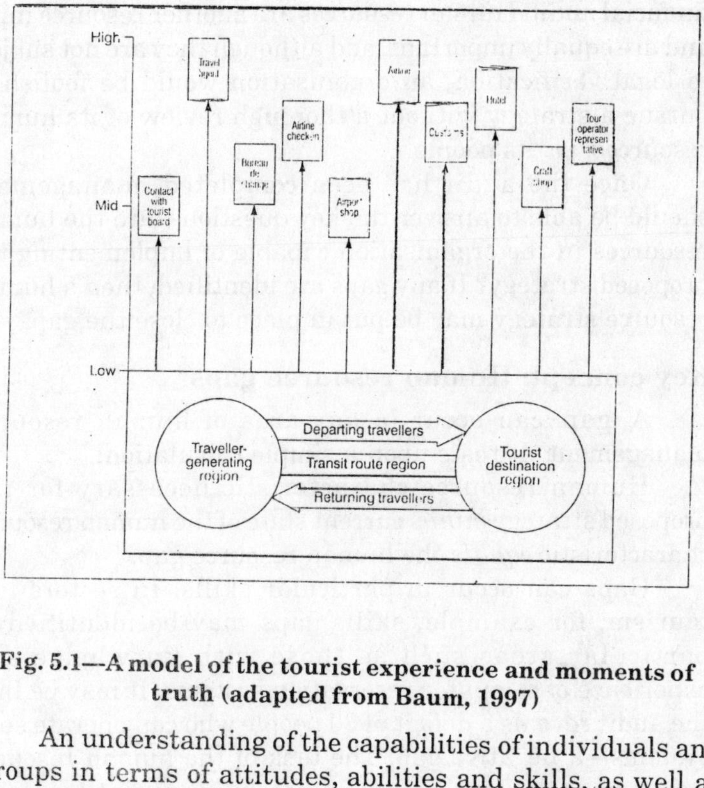

Fig. 5.1—A model of the tourist experience and moments of truth (adapted from Baum, 1997)

An understanding of the capabilities of individuals and groups in terms of attitudes, abilities and skills, as well as an understanding of how individuals relate one to another, is an important part in the preparation and development of strategy. A key 'tool' in gaining an understanding of an organisation's human resources is the human resource audit.

The human resource audit

The purpose of HR audit

The human resource audit is an investigation into the size, skills, structure and all other issues surrounding those currently employed by the organisation. The audit reviews the ability of the human resources to implement a chosen strategy or a range of strategic options.

Most organisations employ accountants to maintain a constant review of financial resources, and each year limited companies subject themselves (by law) to a formal external financial audit. Human resources are another resource input and are equally important, and although they are not subject to legal verification, an organisation would be foolish to pursue a strategy without a thorough review of its human resources, *i.e.* its people.

Once the audit has been completed, management should be able to answer the key question—are the human resources in the organisation capable of implementing the proposed strategy? If any gaps are identified, then a human resource strategy may be put in place to close the gap.

Key concept: Human resource gaps

A 'gap' can occur in any area of human resource management. It rests upon a simple calculation:

Human resource characteristic necessary for the proposed strategy *minus* current state of the human resource characteristic *equals* the human resource gap.

Gaps can occur in particular skills. In sectors like tourism, for example, skills gaps may be identified in particular areas such as those with knowledge and experience of computer reservation systems. It may be that the audit reveals a deficit of 30 people who can operate such systems—a negative gap. The task of the human resource department thus becomes to successfully appoint or retrain to gain the requisite number of skilled operators.

Positive gaps may also be identified—surpluses of a particular type of employee. The human resource strategy thus has to put measures in place to 'dispose' of the excess labour.

Gaps may be closed by using the 'five Rs' individually or in combination. The five Rs are:

- Retirement
- Retraining
- Redeployment
- Redundancy
- Recruitment

The contents of a human resource audit

The contents of a human resource audit may vary from organisation to organisation depending on its size, geographic coverage, and type of activity. However, a typical audit checklist is as follows:

- *The number of employees by a number of counting methods*—the total number, by division, by location, by skill type, by grade or place in hierarchy, by age or length of service, by gender and by ethnic origin.
- *Employee costs*—usually measured by salary costs and 'add-ons' like national insurance, etc.
- The organisational structure and the position of employees within the structure.
- Recruitment and selection procedures and their effectiveness.
- The quality and effectiveness of training and development programmes used.
- The level of employee motivation and morale.
- The nature of employee or industrial relations between management and employees.
- The internal and external networks that employees in the organisation have developed (and their effectiveness for various purposes).
- The monitoring of the effectiveness of existing human resource policies and control procedures.

Formal and informal human resource audits

The information provided by the audit can provide management with important information about the state of the organisations's human resources. In most types of organisation, regular audits are essential to success. However, for a professional soccer club or an orchestra, the state of the human resources is completely transparent and the audit occurs continually—although it may never be formally conducted. A football team that loses every match or an orchestra that sounds terrible will have obvious human resource skill deficits. A formal audit is hardly necessary in such a circumstance.

Formal audits may be carried out by personnel specialists on a regular basis (say annually), or whenever management needs the information for the purposes of a strategic analysis. Practitioners in this area make the point that the simple following of 'lists' like that outlined above, is only a starting point. As points of interest are raised, such as they skill deficiencies, then it is imperative that the reasons for the shortage (or surplus) are also examined as an integral part of the audit.

The outcomes of a human resource audit

The problem of measurement

The various components of a human resource audit present differing problems of quantification. We can intuitively understand that entries like employee costs, numbers, skills shortages or surpluses can be measured in numerical terms. Industrial relations measures can usually be measured by such things as days lost through strikes, etc. Other parts of the audit present more difficulty in respect of measurement.

How, for example, might we measure staff morale or motivation? We might be able to say that staff morale is high or low, but any 'in-between' night be difficult to assign a value to in the same way as for, say, employee costs. The same problems arise with the levels of staff motivation and job satisfaction. It is also probably true to say that in most organisations, large disparities exist between employees in respect of these intangibles. Some employees will be highly motivated and will enjoy good morale whilst others will not. It is for these reasons that a 'checklist' approach to human resource audit is rarely possible—it usually contains some subjective assessments of some parts of the audit.

Human resource benchmarking

The concept of benchmarking is one that we will encounter several times in this book. Essentially, benchmarking is a tool for comparing a feature of one organisation with the same feature of another. It is particularly useful for comparison against the best in an industry for the feature in question. Followers of the best in the industry might then ask why the leader company has achieved the superior performance. Increasingly, however, companies in the service industries are also benchmarking themselves against companies in different sectors, so for example it may be that in the area of offering customer service, hotel companies are able to learn from practices in banking, airlines or car dealers for example.

The feature examined in a benchmarking analysis will depend upon what the organisation needs to know. If, for example, a company identifies a negative gap in a key skill area which it has found difficult to close (say of good quality graduates), a benchmark study will enable the company to find out about its competitors. If Company A is known to be able to attract the best graduates, then an examination of its human resource policies will enable other companies (competitors) to benchmark their own practices against it. It may be that Company A is identified as offering the best career-progression planning, the highest salaries or the best development opportunities. If this is found to be the case, then competitors will want to examine their own provision in these areas to see where they can be improved.

Lead companies may also be analysed for the ways in which they not only manage their internal human resources, but also the ways in which they interact with external sources of labour. Many airlines, for example, close skills gaps by making extensive use of contract workers. They may also 'outsource' some of their work to outside suppliers or use consultants. The ability to attract these 'mobile workers can be just as important as the ability to attract permanent employees.

Identifying human resources as critical success factors

As well as using a human resource audit to identify gaps, it can also be used to establish which, if any, employees or groups of employees are critical to strategic success. These are the people that the organisation's success may have been built upon in the past and it is likely that the existing structures are centred on them.

In some organisations, critical success human resources may be found on the board of directors giving strategic direction to the company as a whole. In others, they might be found in research, developing the new products upon which future success will be built. Certain marketing personnel or operations people might also be critical in some business. For example, in some tour operators, the management of the operational aspects of tours may involve local knowledge and experience of destination areas and individual suppliers. This knowledge and experience may be held by key individuals, whose sudden loss to a company could cause operational problems. Well-managed companies try to reduce this risk through measures such as documented procedures, rotating staff to widen the experience base and training procedures.

Key concept: Critical success factors

It is usually the case that there are one or more reasons why superior performers in an industry are in the positions that they are. These key reasons for success are called *critical success factors* (CSFs). Some companies have uniquely skilled employees, such as particularly skilled engineers or product development specialists. In this case, the CSF is a human resource. In other business, the CSF might be a unique location, a brand image, an enviable reputation, a legally protected patent or licence, a unique production process or technology. This is not to say that other parts of the organisation are unimportant, but merely that the CSF is *the* key cause of the success.

In terms of competitive strategy, the approach to a CSF is to defend it—in some cases at whatever cost it might take. This usually takes to form of 'locking it in' to ensure that the advantage is maintained or that competitors are prevented from gaining the same advantage. If the CSF is in the form of a human resource this might involve contractual arrangements providing financial incentives, long periods of notice to leave the company or providing the right working environment to motivate employees.

The importance of the human resources in a business and the steps that may be taken to motivate and retain key staff is illustrated by the case of Bridge the World.

Motivation and employee retention in Bridge the World

Jerry Bridge, a veteran traveller and top-performing salesman at Trailfinders (a specialist London based travel agency and tour operator), founded the company Bridge the World in London during 1989. It quickly established a niche in the market when it took advantage of the war against Iraq and tumbling air passenger numbers to negotiate good deals with airlines. Since then it has branched out into tailor-made holidays, in which it offers anything from the trip of a lifetime for a retired couple with a pension lump sum to intercontinental adventures for students on a gap year. The company has grown at an annual rate of 23% for the past 10 years, achieving sales of £34 million. The company's employees are important ingredients in this success.

Bright ex-traveller sales staff are employed who are capable of organising complex itineraries and communicating a passion for the product, and they are supported by imaginative marketing. Attracting good staff is not the only challenge. Retaining them is equally important. Despite the growth in sales, profit margins were being eroded because of a haemorrhage of sales staff, with 40% leaving within 15 months of starting. The unacceptably high rate was having a detrimental effect on profitability, not least because sales staff reached peak performance after a year in the job.

Managing Director Jerry Bridge tried to transform the situation by hiring a human resources director and consultants to investigate the problem. A new incentive scheme raised the threshold on sales bonuses and a Bridge the World sabbatical was introduced whereby sales staff who stayed with the company for 21 months qualified for a two-month sabbatical with access to discounted flights and hotels booked through the company. The sabbatical has proved immensely popular among travel-hungry staff, whose average age is 25.

Bridge the World has also sought 'Investors in People' accreditation (a UK government backed training initiative) and spent a lot of money and resources on training. The company now has its own trainer running courses on sales techniques and leadership skills, and has a share ownership scheme for directors and senior management. The company's annual sales staff turnover rate is now 32%, well below the sector's average and still dropping. A combination of measures—money, incentives and training—improved employee retention and performance.

Organisational culture

What is culture?

Culture is the organisational equivalent of a human's personality. As with human personality, organisational culture can be somewhat difficult to explain and define, and consequently many different definitions exist. Ralph Stacey (1996) provided one definition.

> The culture of any group of people is that set of beliefs, customers, practices and ways of thinking that they have come to share with each other through being and working together. It is a set of assumptions people simply accept without question as they interact with each other. At the visible level the culture of a group of people takes the form of ritual behaviour, symbols, myths, stories, sounds and artefacts.

According to Charles Handy, a leading writer on management, the difficulties encountered with defining culture mean that it cannot be precisely defined, for in essence it is 'something that is perceived something felt' (Handy, 1996). Organisational culture can vary enormously from one organisation to another, as Handy pointed out.

Organisations are as different and varied as the nations and societies of the world. They have differing cultures—sets of values and norms and beliefs—reflected in different structures and systems. And the cultures are affected by the events of the past and by the climate of the present, by the technology of the type of work, by their aims and the kind of people that work in them (Handy, 1996).

Culture can thus be explained in terms of the 'feel' of an organisation or its 'character' or as it has sometimes been described as 'the way we do things round here'. Definitions can be a bit inaccessible, but the importance of an organisation's culture lies in the fact that it can be 'felt' whenever it is encountered. From a strategic point of view the important point is that all organisations have culture and that it can have a significant effect upon organisational performance. Consequently, tourism managers must attempt to understand the culture of their organisation and the effect it is having (positive or negative) upon organisational performance. Managers may subsequently find it necessary to take steps to implement a programme that attempts to change the prevailing culture in order to improve performance.

Organisations are as individual as people, and in many ways there are as many cultures as there are organisations—each one is unique. This is not to say, however, that we cannot identify common features between organisational cultures.

The determinants of culture

Why an organisation has a particular type of culture is as complicated a question as asking why a human has a particular personality. It has many possible influences, the net effect of which forge culture over a period of time. Any list would be necessarily incomplete, but following are some of the most important.

- The philosophy of the organisation's founders, especially if the organisation is relatively young.
- The nature of the activities in the business and the character of the industry it competes in.
- The nature of the interpersonal relationship and the nature of industrial or employee relationships.
- The management style adopted and the types of control mechanism—for example, the extent to which management style is autocratic or participative.

- The national or regional character of the areas in which the organisation's activities are located. This, in turn, can affect the power distance, which also influences culture.
- The structure of the organisation, particularly its 'height' and 'width'.
- The dependency the organisation has on technology and the type of technology employed (the growth of e-mail, for example, has had an influence of the culture of some organisations).

Power distance

This is a term attributed to Hickson and Pugh (1995). They use the term to describe 'how removed subordinates feel from superiors in a social meaning of the word "distance". In a high power distance culture, inequality is accepted... in a low power distance culture, inequalities and overt status symbols are minimized and subordinates expect to be consulted and to share decisions with approachable managers'.

Why is culture important?

Culture is important because it can and does affect all aspects of an organisation's activities. The metaphor of human personality may help us to understand this. Some people's personality means they are motivated, sharp, exciting to be with, etc. Others are dull, tedious and apathetic. These personality features will affect all aspects of their lives.

The same is true of an organisation's 'personality'. Culture is important because of the following (not exhaustive) reasons. Culture can have an influence on:

- employee motivation;
- the attractiveness of the organisation as an employer and hence the rate of staff turnover;
- employee morale and 'goodwill';
- productivity and efficiency;
- the quality of work;
- the nature of the employee and industrial relations;
- the attitude of employees in the workplace;
- innovation and creativity.

The point to make after such a list is simply that culture is *very* important. It is essential that management understand the culture of the organisation both in analysing strategic position and then in the implementation of strategy.

The cultural web

On of the most commonly used ways of making sense of an organisation's culture is to use the cultural web (Johnson, 1992). It is a schematic representation of the elements of an organisation's culture in such a way that we can see how each element influences the paradigm.

Key concept: Paradigm

A paradigm is a worldview—a way of looking at the world. It is expressed in the assumptions that people make and in their deep-rooted beliefs. The paradigm of an organisation or a national culture is important because it determines how it will behave in a given circumstance. Given a certain moral dilemma or similar choice, we might expect the paradigms of an orthodox Jew and an atheist Westerner to lead them to arrive at different conclusions. The things that cause one culture to adopt one paradigm and another culture to espouse a different one are set out in the cultural web.

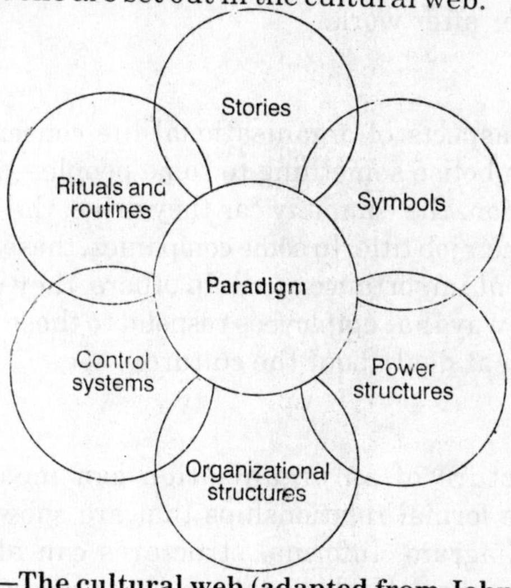

Fig. 5.2—The cultural web (adapted from Johnson, 1992)

The main elements of the web are described below.

Stories

Stories are those narratives that people within the organisation talk to each other about, what they tell new recruits and outsiders about the organisation. The stories typically recount events and people from the past and present—stories of famous victories and defeats. They tend to highlight what is considered important to the members of the organisation.

Routines and rituals

Routines are the procedures for doing things within the organisation. They are repeated on a regular basis to the extent they are taken as 'the way things are done'. Rituals have a longer time frame and can be either formal or informal. Formal routines and rituals are a part of the organisation's practice, such as the 'long service award' or the company. Outward Bound course that work teams might go on from time to time. Informal routines and rituals might include the way that people behave at the annual Christmas party or the extent to which colleagues do (or do not) go for a drink together after work.

Symbols

Symbolic aspects of organisational life concern those things that symbolise something to some people—a certain level of promotion, the company car they drive, the position of their office, their job title. In some companies, these symbols have no apparent importance at all. In others, they matter a great deal. The way that employees respond to these symbols can tell us a great deal about the culture.

Structure

The structure of an organisation can mean more than just those formal relationships that are shown on an organisation diagram. Informal structures can also exist through interpersonal relationships that transcend the formal structures. Some organisations have highly developed informal structures whilst others do not.

Control systems

The ways in which activities are controlled, whether 'tight' or 'loose', is closely aligned to culture. This has a strong link to power distance and the nature of the activities in which the organisation is engaged. Control systems, by definition, concern activity in which performance is gauged against a predetermined standard and the methods of both standard-setting and monitoring performance vary significantly according to culture.

Power structures

The core assumptions that contribute to the paradigm are likely to be made by the most powerful management groupings in the organisation. In some companies, this power resides in the research department, in others it will be the production people or those from another department. In some organisations there may be arguments about what is important between one or more groupings.

Each component of the cultural web exerts its own influence upon the organisation's paradigm. The paradigm describes the aggregate effects of all of the cultural influence on the way the members of the organisation look at the world. This can apply to regions of the world just as it applies to organisations. People indigenous to the Middle East are often thought to have a different view of the world than citizens of countries in north-western Europe. This difference is because of the influence that each component of the cultural web exerts on the national or regional paradigm.

A cultural web for MyTravel plc

MyTravel plc (formerly Airtous plc) is one of the world's leading travel groups with involvement in tour operating, travel retailing, charter airlines, accommo-dation and cruising. Chaired by David Crossland, the business has a corporate headquarters in the Manchester suburbs and other offices elsewhere for its operating divisions. The business was founded in Lancashire some 30 years ago by Crossland, a former travel agency clerk, as a single travel agency .

Stories

- £8000 start-up costs
- David Crossland went from coffee boy to Airtours Chairman
- Consolidation of UK position through takeover of First Choice not allowed
- Difficulties in German subsidiary

Symbols

- David Crossland hard-working family man
- Airtours logo
- Royal blue corporate colour

Power structure

- Head office in Manchester
- Crossland and family, senior management
- Strong management team
- Powerful influences over suppliers

Organisational structure

- Hierarchical
- Team working
- Empowerment of managers to make decisions
- Semi-autonomous divisional offices

Control system

- Economies of scale through central coordination and vertical and horizontal integration
- Partners in joint ventures
- Budgeting, target-setting and financial reporting

Rituals and routines

- Striving for quality
- Importance of advertising and promotion
- Attracting customer loyalty
- Producing 'the brochure'

Paradigm

- Value for money
- Family oriented
- The 'Airtours family'
- Entrepreneurial

Cultural typologies

A number of writers in organisational theory have attempted to group culture types together. The thinking behind such attempts at typology is that if organisations can describe their cultures by type, then this would help in strategic analysis. We will briefly consider two of these attempts.

Handy's culture types

Handy (1996) suggested that organisational cultures could be divided into four broad types: power culture, role cultures, task cultures and person cultures.

Power cultures

This type of organisation is dominated by either a very powerful individual or a dominant small group. It is typified by an organisation that has grown as a result of entrepreneurial flair. Strategic decisions and many operational ones are made by the centre and few decisions are devolved to other managers. As the organisation is dependent on the abilities and personality of the powerful individual, the ability of the organisation to change in response to changes in the environment are sometimes limited by the centre.

Power cultures are common in small entrepreneurial (owner-managed) companies and in some notable larger organisations with a charismatic leader.

Role cultures

This type of culture is found in many long-established organisations that have traditionally operated in stable environments. They tend to be very hierarchical and rely on established procedures, systems and precedent. They often respond slowly to change as it takes time for change to be recognised through the reporting mechanisms. Delays are also encountered in the slow and considered decision-making process.

Role cultures are common in traditional bureaucracies such as the civil service. The task of management in a role culture is to manage procedure. There is usually a high degree of decentralisation and the organisation is run by rules and laid down procedures.

Task cultures

Task cultures are found in organisations engaged in activities of a non-repetitive nature, often high value, one-off tasks. Activities are normally based around flexible multi-disciplinary teams containing expertise in the major disciplines required to complete the project. Teams tend to be small but flexible and find change easy to identify and adjust to. Strategic planning tends to concentrate on the task in-hand.

As their name suggests, task cultures can be found in organisations that are dedicated to a particular task. Consortia that work on large civil engineering projects may demonstrate task culture, as might missionary teams that work together on a medical project in the developing world.

Person cultures

Person cultures are those that exist primarily for the benefit of the members of the organisation itself and hence they tend to be rare in commercial businesses. They can have a very different 'feel' to the other cultures as all members of the organisations work for the benefit of themselves and the other members.

They can be found in learned professional societies, in trade unions, in cooperatives, in some charities and in some religious organisations.

In reality, few organisations fit perfectly into one just classification and they may demonstrate elements of two or more. Some diversified organisations may have divisions that fall into all the categories and the cultures may change over time. Many start as power cultures and then tend towards a role culture as size increases.

In assessing the appropriateness of the four cultural types Lynch (2000) suggested that three criteria might be used. Does the dominant culture identified:

- Fit with prescriptive or emergent forms of strategy formulation?
- Deliver competitive advantage for the organisation?
- Have the ability to cope with strategic change?

Lynch's conclusions are shown in Table.

Table 5.1—An assessment of Handy's four cultural types

	Prescriptive or emergent strategy	**Delivery of competitive advantage**	**Ability to cope with strategic change**
Power culture	Prescriptive	Enhanced but individuals may miss competitive moves	Depends on individual or group at centre
Role culture	Prescriptive	Solid, slow and substantive	Slow, will resist change
Task culture	Emergent	Good where flexibility is important	Accepted and welcomed
Person	Possibly emergent	Depends on individual	Depends on individual

Source : adapted from Lynch (2000 : 319)

In assessing the four main cultural types however, three important qualifications should be made:

1. Organisations change over time.
2. Several types or variations of culture often exist in the same organisation.

3. Different cultures may predominate depending on the headquarters and ownership of the company.

Miles and Snow's culture types

Miles and Snow (1978) categorised cultures into four types, based on how they tend to react in strategic terms.

Defenders

These organisations tend to seek a competitive advantage in terms of targeting niche markets through cost reduction and specialisation. They tend to operate in stable, mature markets and, as the name suggests, they favour defending their current market share by service improvements or further cost savings. Defenders therefore tend to be centralised, have rigid control systems and a hierarchical management structure that does not enjoy sudden change.

Prospectors

These organisations enjoy the challenge of developing and introducing new product to the marketplace. They actively seek out new markets for their products. These favoured strategic require the organisation to constantly monitor the environment and be willing and able to respond to quickly to changes that may occur. To that end, these organisations are decentralised and flexible.

Analysers

These organisations are 'followers' and are conservative in nature. Steady growth through market penetration is the favoured option as this can be achieved without radical changes to structure. Moves into new markets and products only occur after extensive evaluation and market research. They learn from the mistakes of others and tend to balance power between the centre and divisions with complex control systems.

Reactors

Reactors are a bit like analysers in that they tend to follow rather than innovate. They differ from analysers in that they are less conservative and sometimes behave impulsively, having failed fully to consider the implications of their actions. These organisations may lack proper control systems and typically have a weak but dominant leader.

Organisational culture at Southwest Airlines

The culture of Southwest Airlines, which emphasizes employees as the airline's 'first customers' and passengers as the second, has been integral to Southwest Airlines' success. Dallas-based Southwest grew significally during the 1990s and continues to do so, drawing in thousands of employees new to the airline's ways and raising questions about whether it can keep its culture intact. In 1990, the airline had 8600 on its payroll, which rose to about 29 000 employees in 2002, and almost half of these have been with the company less than five years. The airline also has flown beyond its Texas roots into other regions of the USA. Ten years ago it served 31 cities, five years ago 45 and today 56. Southwest is finding that it must work differently to make sure its culture endures. In an attempt to address this, a committee focusing on new employees was created. As turnover edges up an internal branding campaign reminds employees of the 'freedoms' that working at Southwest brings. The airline also is in the relatively new position of having to search for applicants rather than waiting for candidates to come to it.

It takes a lot of hard work to maintain the culture but the airline regularly finds a place towards the top of Fortune magazine's annual list of the 100 best companies to work for in America, the rankings for which are partly determined by employee comments. Southwest's charismatic leader, 69-year-old Herb Kelleher, has devoted much time and energy to creating and maintaining the company's distinctive corporate culture.

Southwest, which began operating in 1971, now challenges the major North American airlines such as American, United and Delta. Originally offering flights in a triangle between Dallas, San Antonio and Houston, the idea of offering fares so cheap that people would abandon their cars for jets has proved very attractive to consumers and has been widely copied. The airline's core offering is to offer lots of short flights between pairs of cities, though in recent years it has been offering more long flights. Reinforcing the low fares is a culture of relaxed professionalism which includes flight attendants who might crack jokes or burst into song. The airline also has neither assigned seats nor a meal service.

Southwest's employees appear to understand what's made the airline succeed. This provides a clarity of purpose at Southwest that makes it easy to retain the culture while growing. In recent years, the airline has added between one and three destinations a year while it has continued to increase the number of flights from its existing cities such as Houston.

Employees get four cards a year from the company: for birthdays, a December holiday, Valentine's Day and the company anniversary day. Throughout the company, employees are encouraged to hold 'celebrations' to mark birthdays, engagements and other milestones. Creativity also is emphasized, especially when it comes to finding relief in high-stress jobs. Customer relations workers may come to work in pyjamas for a day. Profit sharing ties employees directly to company performance. Southwest built an infrastructure that ensures that when an employee does something good, the whole organisation knows about it. The lives of Southwest employees, along with the company's history, are highlighted on the headquarters' walls.

To help facilitate communications a 'culture committee' was established in 1990 aiming to do what was necessary to create, enhance and enrich the Southwest spirit. In one way or another the committee tries to ensure that fellow workers are appreciated and that people appreciate the difficulties involved with other people's positions. Local culture committees have also been established in cities across Southwest's network. A committee focusing on new employees has also been added in order to make sure that new employees are inducted appropriately and receive proper guidance and mentoring during their early careers. The company is paying more attention to employee retention as turnover creeps up. For a long time it was 5-7%, but it increased to 9.8% in 1999. An internal branding campaign has been established which identifies eight basic freedoms of working at Southwest. Employees, the company says, get the freedom to: pursue good health; travel; learn and grow; stay connected; have financial security; work and have fun; make a pcsitive difference; and be creative and innovative.

6

The Travel and Tourism Organisation—Financial Analysis and Performance Indicators

Introduction

The ability to make sense of an organisation's financial situation is an important part of strategic analysis. In order to carry out a financial analysis of a company's situation or of an industry, it is necessary to understand some of the fundamentals of finance and its sources. This chapter begins with a discussion of the sources of corporate finance and then goes on to discuss the costs of the various types of capital. This information helps students to make sense of a company's financial structure before the tools of conventional financial analysis are discussed. The various 'tools' for financial analysis are introduced and, finally, the concept of bench-making is explained and its use in analysis is discussed.

Learning Objectives

After studying this chapter, students should be able to:

- understand what is meant by financial analysis;
- identify the sources of funds available to companies and the relative advantages and disadvantages of each;

- assess a company's potential for further funding based on current position, future prospects and past performance;
- explain the cost and non-cost issues involved in raising and using various forms of capital;
- understand the importance of the cost of capital;
- describe the limitations of a company report and accounts as a source of data for financial analysis;
- describe the major tools that can be used to analyse a company's financial position;
- explain the nature and analysis of foreign exchange risks in travel and tourism;
- understand the nature and analysis of cash flow risks in travel and tourism.

An introduction to financial analysis

The importance of finance

Although the travel and tourism industry covers a diversity of different organisations, including tour operators, airlines hotels and travel agencies, financial management is important to all of them. Financial management is that part of the total management function concerned with the effective and efficient raising and use of funds. Finance, like a physical resource, has a large number of competing uses; is scarce but can be obtained at a price; and is bought and sold in markets. Financial management is concerned with managing this scarce resource so as to ensure that:

- sufficient *finance* is available at the right time;
- *finance* is obtained at the least possible cost;
- *finance* is used in the most profitable ways.

Most university business courses have an accounting and finance content. You may consequently be familiar with some of the content of this chapter and this will be to your advantage. This chapter develops the material into the context of strategic analysis.

Money, or the lack of it, is central to the strategic development of all organisations, large or small. It is one of the key resource inputs and cannot be ignored. The most original strategies and the most complex plans for the future of a business are meaningless unless management has considered the financial position of the organisation at the outset and during the period covered by the strategy. The ability of a company to finance both current and future strategies is central to any analysis of the company's position. A central theme to this chapter will be the ability of the company to finance current strategies—its ability to raise the funding required for future developments.

The success or failure of the organisation is judged by its ability to meet its strategic objectives. The financial information (in the form of annual corporate reports) produced by companies provides a quantifiable means of assessing success. It is important to recognise, however, that other quantifiable information, such as efficiency and productivity data, and non-quantifiable data such as the company's image, can also be used to make such judgements. In this chapter we will examine the value of information extracted from corporate reports as a source from which judgements can be made.

Corporate reports are, however, just one source of information about a company's financial state. Managers have a number of ways of gathering information about their own and competitors' finances and we will discuss these later in the chapter. The case of the UK tour operator International Leisure Group (ILG) illustrates the pitfalls that overcome an organisation when management makes strategic errors in the financial management of a company.

International Leisure Group (ILG)

Flying too close to the sun—anatomy of a corporate collapse

The ILG group of companies, like Icarus from Greek mythology, flew too close to the sun, got burnt and fell to earth. We can focus on four aspects of ILG and its demise.

1. The company

ILG was formed in the early 1970s by the extrovert, publicity seeking Harry Goodman. It traded under various brand names, including Intasun, Club 18-30, Lancaster tour operators and the airline Air Europe. The company grew rapidly throughout the 1970s and 1980s, spurred on by Britain's apparently insatiable appetite for package holidays, the number of which trebled during the 1980s. The company was also helped by the collapse of Clarkson's, the UK's second largest tour operator, in 1974 and Laker Airways eight years after, both of which 'Harry' took full advantage of.

The growth in company sales (which in its last published figures for 1989 had a turnover of approximately £722 million) was not matched by a corresponding growth in profits and its gearing levels were extremely high.

After a relatively brief life as quoted company, the management team led by Harry Goodman took the company 'private' in the spring of 1987. The stock market, it was said, took too short term a view of the company. A Swiss financier took a 49% holding in the company, which was reduced to 29.5% in 1990.

2. The strategy

ILG's financial strategy was simple. It used cash generated from its travel and charter airline businesses to finance the development of a new scheduled airline. The tour operations certainly worked on very tight margins (thanks in part to the price war Goodman himself had started in 1985), but tour operations also produced a good cash flow. Advance payments from customers (which usually stood at about £50 million) provided a source of interest-free funding.

The company was to have been a pan-European airline based on modern fuel efficient aircraft and taking advantage of Europèan airline deregulation in the 1990s. Cash was also provided by the group's third, less visible business, trading in aircraft. By placing orders for new aircraft several years ahead, the company was at the head of the queue in the mid 1980s when aircraft demand was high. Consequently the company could sell aircraft at a profit. This source provided a third of operating profits in 1989.

3. The faults

Although tour operations provided a good cash flow, it was, nevertheless, fundamentally a high volume, low margin business trying to finance a highly volatile airline development. The costs of developing the airline were considerable and were much higher than had been planned.

To develop the airline, the company negotiated inventive leasing arrangements with a handful of banking syndicates, the largest led by Citibank accounting for 10 of the company's 37 aircraft.

The first apparent weakness, then, was that in return for narrow lending margins, the banks insisted on onerous covenants (financial restrictions) and these were to prove crucial later. A second apparent weakness was an over-commitment by Lloyds Bank. Lloyds began with a £30 million working capital facility but eventually had up to £90 million at risk. A third financial weakness existed in the financial team. Goodman was highly autocratic, but his flair was largely marketing based rather than financial. Beneath him the company appeared to lack an obvious financial strategist. A fourth financial weakness was that the management was also firmly entrenched. They had only 15% of the equity but 100% of ordinary voting shares (Goodman with 53%), giving them a blocking vote.

4. The collapse

By spring 1990 Goodman had already decided that the company should be sold. Some approaches were made but nothing materialised. At the end of October 1990 ILG breached the strict covenants agreed in spite of a £22 million injection of funds by the Swiss investors. The banks gave three months for the company to sort out the problems.

However, bookings in the crucial pre-Christmas period were poor with the onset of recession (down an estimated 20% on the already poor level of 1989). The Gulf War in the New Year was disastrous for package bookings, which were down 40% on a year earlier and scheduled services were operating at 35% capacity.

The writing seemed to be on the wall, but a last minute deal was agreed at the end of January with £40 million of cash from the Swiss and Lloyds converting £50 million of debt into equity. By mid February it was clear that this would not be enough. The Swiss investors were themselves in trouble. Lloyds then agreed to an additional £20 million with a further £20 million from a German investor. In early March the German investor pulled out and a syndicate of banks led by Citibank took steps to have 10 of Air Europe's aircraft 'arrested'. The following day the company was placed in administration.

The company, bought out largely with funds provided by the banks, found in the end that the banks would not support it, was ILG's flawed financial structure that was its real undoing.

Understanding financial structure

At the outset it is necessary to have an understanding of a business's financial structure. A company's annual accounts will contain two key statements: the balance sheet and the statement of profit and loss. We will examine each briefly.

Understanding the balance sheet

Assets are financed (and matched in the balance sheet) by capital and liabilities. Liabilities may be current (less than one year) or long term (over one year).

Capital + Liabilities = Assets

The principles underpinning a balance sheet are shown in Fig. 6.1.

In Fig. 6.1 the assets of the business are 'funded' by long-term funds (capital), comprising such items as long-term loans, share capital and reserves. Current liabilities comprise items such as overdrafts and trade creditors.

A proportion of the short-term assets are funded by long-term funding, which, unlike short-term funding (current liabilities), is difficult to take away at short notice and consequently represents a more stable form of financing. Overdrafts, for example, can be quickly recalled by banks if they choose to do so.

Long-term (or fixed) assets such as property, land, vehicles and aircraft are financed entirely by more stable financing sources, *i.e.* long-term funding.

The difference between current assets (stock, debtors and cash) and current liabilities (creditors, overdrafts and short-term loans) is the company's 'working capital' (net current assets).

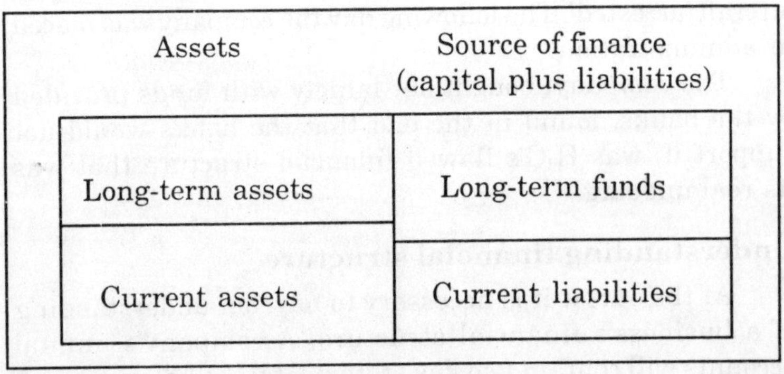

Fig. 6.1—A representation of the principles of a balance sheet.

A skeleton balance sheet is shown below:

	Item	£	Examples
A	Fixed assets	80	Semi permanent assets—property, plant, vehicles, aircraft etc.
B	Current assets	40	Trading assets—stock, debtors, cash
C	Current liabilities	(20)	Trading liabilities—creditors, overdrafts
	Net current assets (working capital B-C)	20	
	Total capital employed (A + B – C)	**100**	
D	Shareholder finance	75	Share capital, retained profits
E	Long term liabilities	25	Medium-and long-term loans
	Sources of finance (D + E)	**100**	

Understanding the profit and loss account

A profit and loss (P&L) account matches the revenue earned in a period with the costs incurred in earning it. A skeleton profit and loss account is shown below:

	Sales or income received
Less	Cost of sales
Equals	Gross profit
Less	Expenses (such as personnel costs, head office costs, administration and distribution)
Equals	Profit before interest and tax (also called operating, trading or 'net' profit)
Less	Interest and tax
Equals	Profit after interest and tax (also called earnings)
Less	Dividends to shareholders
Equals	Retained profit (which is transferred to the balance sheet).

Sources of corporate funding

Financial resources, as we have already learned, are an essential input to strategic development. Capital for development can be raised from several sources and these are summarised here.

Key concept: Capital

Accountants use the term capital to describe one particular type of 'money'. It is usually contrasted with revenue. *Revenue* is money that is earned through normal business transactions—through sales, rents or whatever the company 'does' through its normal activities. *Capital* is money that is used to invest in the business—to buy new equipment, new capacity, extra aircraft, etc. The investment of capital enables the business to expand and, through that expansion, to increase its revenue and profits in future years. Capital can be raised from shareholders, through retained profits, through rights issues, through loan capital or through the disposal of assets.

Share capital

For limited companies, a sizeable proportion of capital is raised from shareholders (the financial owners of the company) in the form of share capital.

Historically, share capital has comprised the majority of capital for a limited company's start-up and subsequent development. In return for their investment, shareholders receive a return in accordance with the company's performance in a given year in the form of a dividend. The dividend per share is taken as an important measure by shareholders of the company's success in its chosen strategy. Shares also confer on their holders a right to vote on company resolutions at annual or extraordinary company meetings *pro rata* with the proportion of their holding. It follows of course that a shareholding in excess of 50% confers total control over a company's strategy.

Under normal circumstances, share capital is considered to be permanent—it is not paid back by the company. It is thus unlike other forms of capital (*e.g.* loan capital). The shareholders' only 'payback' is in the form of dividends and thrcugh capital growth—an increase in the value of the shares. Shareholders who wish to divest their stock (*i.e.* shareholding) in a company must usually sell it *via* a stock exchange (in the case of shares in a public limited company) or through a private sale (in the case of a private company). In exceptional circumstances, some companies offer a 'buyback' of their own shares.

Shareholders can be individuals or 'institutional shareholders'. Some individuals hold their personal share portfolio but the vast majority of shares are held by institutional shareholders such as pension funds, life assurance companies and investment trusts. The profile of shareholders varies from company to company and from country to country.

Concepts : Share value and share volume

Share value is the price of a given company's shares at a given point in time. Like any other commodity, its value is determined by the forces of supply and demand. Given that in normal circumstances the supply is fixed over the short to medium term, price is determined by how many people want to buy it. If the market has confidence in a company's prospects, demand for the share will rise and so, accordingly, will its price. If a company's prospects are considered poor, investors will sell the share, fewer will want to buy it and the price will fall.

Share volume is the number of shares issued by a company in total. This is usually determined at the foundation or flotation of a company although rights issues and similar events can increase the share volume. It is generally true that larger companies have higher share volumes than smaller concerns.

Rights issue capital

From time to time, a company may seek to increase its capital for expansion by means of a *rights issue.* This is when a company issues new shares to the stock market, normally giving its own shareholders the first refusal *pro rata* with their current proportion of the company's share volume.

The decision to go for a rights issue may well be a strategic decision for management because it can impact on the ownership of the company. If existing shareholders do not exercise their right to buy, then it is likely that ownership will be diluted, *i.e.* shareholders will find that they own a lower percentage of share volume than they used to.

Those shares not taken up by shareholders, who may be unable or unwilling to buy them, are normally covered by *underwriters* (institutional investors) at a price agreed, in advance. Underwriting is an important technical feature of new share issues and as such is a major cost in the process. A rights issue is sometimes seen as a reward to loyal shareholders.

A variation on a rights issue is *placing.* A placing involves the selling of shares direct to a small number of investors, usually large financial institutions. This may be marginally cheaper than a rights issue, but its major advantage is its flexibility in enabling new shareholders to have significant and possibly strategic holdings. Placings take place, for example, as a part of a joint venture agreement whereby the two companies exchange placed shareholdings as a sign of their mutual commitment to the alliance.

Retained profit as a source of capital

Shareholders provide other funds for development by agreeing *not* to receive all the company's profits in a given year. *Retained profit,* that element of operating profit not paid to shareholders in the form of dividend, is the most common method of funding strategic developments, particularly if the company is quite old in terms of years. By using this form of funding, organisations save on the costs involved in using alternatives such as fees to merchant banks, lawyers and accountants. It also means management do not have to reveal nor justify their strategies to others and risk their plans becoming known to competitors.

It should be recognised that retained profits do not constitute a loss to shareholders as such, because the value of the organisation and consequently the share price is normally increased when these funds are used for reinvestment. It is, however, important that companies recognise the need to balance the proportion of profits distributed and retained in order to satisfy those shareholders who need regular funds flow themselves (such as insurance and pension companies).

Loan capital

An important consideration in the use of retained profits to find corporate development is clearly the ability of the company actually to make a profit than can be, at least in part, distributed to shareholders as dividends. Whilst a company may make a profit from its normal activities after taxation, some profits may be required to meet the cost of other forms of debt finance or loans.

Debt finance is shown in the balance sheet under two headings, *Creditors: amounts following within one year* and *Creditors: amounts falling due after more than one year.* The form of borrowing with most impact on strategic development is that falling due after more than one year—long-term debt. This type of borrowing can take a number of forms. In addition to the use of long-term bank loans, a company can use debentures, convertible loan stock or corporate bonds.

Debt finance is normally for a set period of time and at a fixed rate of interest. The interest must be paid every year, regardless of the level of profit (referred to as *servicing* the debt). The interest rate for this source is normally less than the cost of share capital (when the dividend payable on the shares is taken into account).

Comparing share capital and loan capital

Each of the types of capital described above has its *pros and cons*. Share capital has the advantage that the amount paid on the capital is dependent upon company results. A company can decide not to pay a dividend if profits are poor in any given year. Loan capital, by contrast, must be serviced regardless of results in much the same way that a mortgage on a house must be repaid regardless of other commitments.

Offsetting this advantage is the fact that share capital is permanent. As long as the company exists, it has an obligation to repay a dividend to its shareholders. Loan capital has the advantage to the company that it is time-limited. Servicing the capital is restricted to the term of the loan (like a mortgage on a house) and when it is finally repaid in full, the business has no further obligation to the lender.

The fact that the repayment of debt finance takes precedence over dividends on shares means that shareholders bear an increased risk. If the company performs badly, their return on investment will be small or non-existent in a given year. Against this possibility, they usually expect to receive higher returns compared to providers of loan capital in the years when profits are good.

The major advantages and disadvantages of share and loan capital are set out in Table 6.1.

Table 6.1—Summary of the major advantages and disadvantages of share and loan capital

	Advantages	Disadvantages
Share capital	No fixed charge or legal obligation to pay a dividend No maturity date Issue of equity increases credit worthiness Marketable, *i.e.* can be traded	Extension of voting rights High issue costs May increase average cost of capital Dividends not tax deductible
Loan capital	Known and often lower cost No dilution of equity Interest payable is tax deductible	Increase in risk which may cause value of equity to fall Need for repayment Limit to amount of available funding

In practice, business profits can vary significantly over time. In some years, it is preferable to use loan capital, especially when interest rates are low and profits are high. In other years, when profits are lower and interest rates are higher, share capital works out cheaper. The fact that the benefits are so finely divided means that most companies opt to use an element of both. The relationship of debt capital to shareholder capital is referred to as the company's *gearing ratio*.

Gearing is an indication of how the company has arranged its capital structure. It can be expressed as either:

$$\frac{\text{Borrowed capital (\textit{i.e.} debt)}}{\text{Total capital employed (\textit{i.e.} borrowings plus shareholders' capital)}}$$

or, as

$$\frac{\text{Borrowed capital } (i.e. \text{ debt})}{\text{Shareholders' capital } (i.e. \text{ equity})}$$

Both are usually expressed as percentages by simply multiplying the quotient by 100. It is not important which one is used unless we are comparing the gearing of two or more companies.

Other sources of capital

Whilst the foregoing are the most common mechanisms of raising capital for development, others are available under some circumstances. One such method is to dispose of existing fixed assets. This can range from selling of an aircraft to selling a subsidiary to a third party.

Finally, marginal improvements in a company's capital situation can be achieved by improving the management of working capital. Over the course of a financial year, small savings can accumulate to significant proportions, increasing both profitability and capital for reinvestment. This can be achieved by:

- extending the time taken to pay creditors;
- getting debtors to pay sooner; or,
- spreading payments through leasing rather than purchasing assets.

Working capital is the amount of money that a company has tied up in the normal operation of its business. Working capital comprises money tied up in:

- stocks;
- debtors (money owed to the business);
- creditors (money the company owes);
- cash or current bank deposits.

A company's objective is usually to minimize this figure, or to manage the working capital in such a way that minimizes financing costs or maximizes earnings on cash balances. This is an important source of earnings for many travel and tourism companies.

Working capital is needed to pay for goods, services and expenses before money can be recovered from creditors.

The ability of a business to pay its cash commitments as they fall due shows that it has sufficient *liquidity*.

Inefficient management of working capital can lead to over-investment in working capital—*over-capitalisation*. Conversely *under-capitalisation,* also known as overtrading, often occurs when a company tries to do too much, too soon with too little long-term capital. A company can be trading profitably but run out of cash to make payments, *i.e.* it can become *insolvent*. Warning signs of overtrading include: a rapid increase in sales, a rapid increase in current assets, small increase in share capital, a deterioration in liquidity ratios such as the acid test ratio which measures the proportion of current assets less stocks to current liabilities.

Cost of capital

Definitions

Availability of capital (where to get it from) is one issue when examining a company's capital funding, but another equally important consideration is its cost. We learned above that providers of loans or share capital (equity) both require a return on their investments. Management therefore need to know what return (profit) they need to make in order to meet the minimum requirements of capital providers. Failure to achieve this minimum will make the raising of future funds all the more difficult. The cost of capital can be seen as the minimum return required on the company's assets, which in turn may influence the objectives of the company.

At its simplest, the cost of capital can be viewed as the annual amount payable (as a percentage) against the principal amount of money. Most of us will be aware that the return payable on such things as loans varies between lenders and over time as interest rates rise or fall. The cost of loans on a credit card is, for example, much higher than a mortgage loan (where the security against the loan is mainly responsible for the difference). Some fortunate people are able to borrow money interest-free (at zero cost of capital).

Cost of debt capital

The costs of debt capital are relatively easy to calculate as they tend to correspond closely to the prevailing rate of interest. If the loan is to be repaid at a fixed rate, the calculation is even more straightforward. It is generally the case that the rate of interest attached to a loan will be strongly influenced by the risk of default. Unsecured loans attract the highest rates whilst those that can be recovered by the sale of the asset against which the loan is taken out (such as a property) will attract a lower rate. The history of the business in dealing with lenders (its credit rating) will also be a factor.

Cost of share capital

Calculating the cost of share capital is slightly more complex as it contains more variables. Acconting academics spend a great deal of time discussing what should and should not be included in this calculation and how each component should be weighted. Reasons for this complexity include the indefinite nature of the funding, the opportunity cost of undistributed profits and shareholders' expectations. These mean that some models try to include components for inflation, industry averages and attitudes towards risk.

At its simplest, the cost of share capital can be calculated as follows:

Cost of share capital (equity) as a percentage =

$$\frac{\text{Current net dividend per share}}{\text{Current market price of share}} \times 100$$

$$+ \text{ average percentage annual growth rate}$$

Example

If the market price for shares were 400p per share and the annual dividend was 20p. If growth in profits average 10% per annum, this gives

Cost of share capital = 20/400 × 100 + 10%
= 15%

Models of capital costing

The CAPM model

The *Capital Asset Pricing Model* (CAPM) is a more complex but widely this model used for calculating the cost of share capital.

Cost of share capital = Ri + β (Rm - Ri)

The model takes into account the competitor financial products available to potential investors. These range from the percentage return on virtually risk free government bonds (Ri) to a component covering the average interest for the share (equity) markets overall (Rm). The final element of the model represents the company itself, or more correctly its position relative to the market overall. The β coefficient is a measure of the volatility of the company's financial returns.

The CAPM model does have a number of drawbacks, which need to be recognised. First, the shares of the company need to be traded on a stock market. This means that the cost of equity in private companies cannot be calculated using this model. Secondly the volatility of share prices in recent years causes problems in arriving at a date for 'acceptable' returns. The dynamic and complex nature of many industries and markets also suggest that historical data has limited value.

Example: CAPM model

Assume that risk free government bonds were trading at 4% and the average return on the market was 10%. Also assume that the volatility of the company had been calculated at 1.1, (meaning the shares fluctuated slightly more than the market average).

Cost of share capital (equity) = 4% + 1.1 (10% – 4%) = 10.6%

The WACC model

Whereas the CAPM model is used to calculate the cost of share capital, the *Weighted Average Cost of Capital*

(WACC) can be used to determine the overall cost of funding to a company. The calculation of this information is relatively simple.

WACC = (Proportion of loan finance × Cost of loan finance) + (Proportion of shareholders' funds × Cost of shareholders' funds)

Example: WACC model

Assume that a company had £30 million of loan capital and £70 million equity funding. The cost of each type had been calculated as 5% and 15% respectively, the calculation would be as follows:

Type of capital	Proportion	Cost (after tax)	Weighted cost
Loan finance	0.3	5%	1.5%
Shareholders' funds	0.7	15%	10.5%
Total	1.0		12.0%

Why calculate the cost of capital?

The cost of capital is usually an important figure to calculate because if it works out to be too high, the development that it is intended to fund may not be viable. Given that both debt and share capital attract servicing costs, the profit returns must exceed these servicing costs to the extent that the proposal is economically attractive.

If the projected returns on a strategic development (such as a new factory facility) are not much more than the projected servicing costs, then management will have to make a judgement as to whether the investment is actually 'worth the risk'.

The whole situation is rendered more complex if debt capital is obtained at a variable rate of interest. Interest rates can vary substantially throughout an economic cycle and depend upon such things as government inflation targets, the currency exchange value and the national rate of capital deposition.

There are no guidelines as to the ideal capital structure—the balance between debt and equity finance. The optimal structure will vary from company to company, from industry to industry and from year to year. Some companies will calculate their WACC and include factors which are difficult to quantify, such as the degree of risk faced by the industry trends in interest rates and even the cost and availability of funds to competitors.

Financial analysis

The basics

We would usually employ an analysis of a company's financial situation as part of an internal strategic analysis. We may wish to understand a company's finances in order to make an assessment of its 'health' or its readiness to undertake a phase of strategic development.

Three key areas of financial analysis are:

- longitudinal analysis (sometimes called trend analysis);
- cross-sectional analysis (or comparison analysis);
- ratio analysis.

A comprehensive analysis of a company's financial situation would normally involve an element of all three of these analyses. The one thing to bear in mind when looking at accounting statements is that they contain numbers in isolation. An accounting number on it own is just that—a number. In order to make any sense of it, we must compare it with other accounting numbers. In the next few sections Air New Zealand will be used to illustrate some of the 'tools' of financial analysis. Air New Zealand is an airline providing services to, from and within New Zealand, Australia and the South West Pacific. In June 2000 Air New Zealand achieved full ownership of the Australian carrier Ansett, giving the combined Air New Zealand —Ansett Group, which is a member of the 'Star' strategic alliance, the scale of a world top 20 airline. Note, the airline subsequently sold its Ansett stake.

To many organisations in travel and tourism two further areas of finance are key to considering the overall financial situation, namely analyses of the organisation's exposure to:

- foreign exchange risks analysis;
- cash flow risk analysis.

Longitudinal analysis

The simplest means of assessing any aspect of a company's finances is to compare the data for two or more years and see what has increased and what has decreased over that time period, and by how much. It goes without saying that the longer back in time we look, then the better idea we will get as to the organisation's current position in its historical context (see for example Fig. 6.2). Many company corporate reports provide a five or ten years record and this can help us in constructing a longitudinal analysis.

The easiest way to perform this form of analysis is conduct an initial scan of the figures to identify any major changes between the years. This involves simply looking along each line in turn, and highlighting any larger than normal increases or decreases, for example a scan along five years of fuel expenses shown below clearly indicates that large increases in these costs occurred over the period 1996 to 2000 and particularly between the years 1999 and 2000.

Year	2000	1999	1998	1997	1996
Fuel costs (NZ$000)	464	322	347	356	318

Anomalies like these may need further investigation. The impact of the 'blip' on the year's performance must be assessed as must its impact on current performance. Further investigation of the balance sheet or profit and loss account, together with any notes to the accounts, may provide some clues.

The initial scan may need to be followed by a more detailed analysis, which might, for example, calculate the year on year increase / decrease in percentage terms. It is sometimes helpful to plot trends on a graph against time (such as in Figure 6.2). This can help to highlight changes at particular points in time.

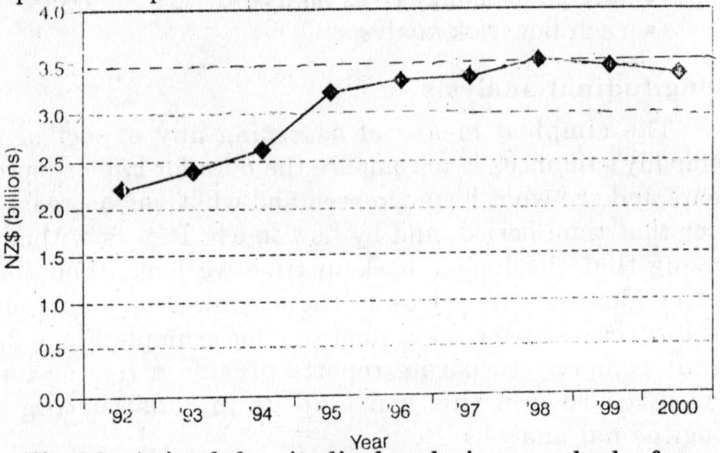

Fig. 6.2—A simple longitudinal analysis: annual sales for Air New Zealand (1992-2000)

The identification of trends, in terms of say turnover, costs or of some items of a balance sheet (such as debtors) can therefore be valuable in our financial analysis. such trends should, however, be seen in their context. An organisation operating in a static or slow growth market may judge a 1% year on year increase in turnover as a great success, whereas for a company in a buoyant market would judge a 1% increase as a failure.

Cross-sectional analysis

Whilst longitudinal analysis helps us to assess performance against a historical trend, it tells us nothing of the company's performance against that of competitors or of companies in other industries. If we were, for example, to identify strong sales growth of 10% a year in a longitudinal analysis of Company A's financial statements, we might be tempted to think that the company was performing well. If we were then to compare this company with one of its competitors only to find that the industry average rate of growth was 15%, then we would wish to modify our initial assessment of Company A's performance.

Intercompany comparison or financial *benchmarking* is a variation on cross-sectional analysis. It usually involves an analysis of 'like' companies, usually in the same industry but it can occasionally be an inter-industry analysis.

In order to make the benchmarking analysis meaningful, the company selection should usually be guided by similarity by:

- company size (*i.e.* they should be comparable in terms of turnover, market value or similar);
- industry (in that the companies produce similar products);
- market (*i.e.* the companies share a similar customer base).

In practice, sample selection for benchmarking study always involves some compromise because no two companies are in all respects directly comparable. Many companies, for example, operate in more than one industry and this may render problematic any comparisons with another company that operates in only one industry.

Accountants and financial analysts have undertaken the practice of inter-company (cross-sectional) analysing using financial data for many years. Benchmarking, however, can be used to compare financial and, importantly, non-financial information between two or more companies.

Benchmarking is now used to compare the effectiveness of various processes, products and procedures against others. The objective is to identify where superior performance is found in whatever variable that is being used for comparison. Once the company with the highest performance is identified, the exercise becomes to explore the reasons behind the superior performance.

The benchmarking process therefore involves decisions on:

- What are we going to benchmark? (financial or non financial data)
- Who are we going to benchmark against? (sample selection)
- How will we get the information?
- How will we analyse the information?
- How will we use the information?

The value of benchmarking is in identifying not only which company has the superior performance in a sector but also why this is the case. Our analysis, for example, might highlight the fact that Company X enjoys a return on sales significantly higher than the other companies in the sector. Company X thus occupies the profitability benchmark in the sector. The other companies may then wish to examine the practices within Company X that give rise to this level of performance.

For non-financial indicators, our analysis may highlight the fact that Company Y is able to attract the best-qualified people within a key category of personnel, for example the best scientists or computer programmers. In this case, Company Y demonstrates the benchmark in successful recruitment. Other companies who are unable to attract the best personnel would usually wish to examine Company Y to see why it is so successful in this regard.

Commonly sized accounts are particularly useful in cross-sectional analyses but it can also be used to analyse the same company's accounts from year to year. If we were, for example, to examine the P&L or balance sheets of two companies in the same industry, we may at first be unable to make sense of differences between the two. We can sometimes make sense of the two separate accounts by making the totals of both equal 100 and then dividing each entry by the resultant quotient accordingly. A simplified example of commonly sized accounts is shown in Table 6.2.

Table 6.2 —Simplified profit and loss accounts for two hypothetical companies

	Company A		Company B	
	£m	Common size	£m	common size
Sales	113.4	100	224.6	100
Cost of sales	65.0	57.32	112	49.87
Gross profit	48.4	42.68	112.6	50.13
Administrative and other costs	33.7	29.72	67.0	29.83
Operating profit	14.7	12.96	45.6	20.3

From Table 6.2, we can make comparisons between the cost structures of the two companies despite the fact that Company B has approximately twice the turnover of Company A. We can tell, for example, that overall, Company B is better at controlling overall costs that Company A evidenced by the fact that its operating profit is 20.3 compared to Company A's figure of 14.7. We could draw comparable conclusions from other commonly sized components of the accounts.

Concept: Financial statements

One of the conditions placed upon limited companies is the requirement to file an audited annual report and accounts. There are five compulsory components to this document as set out in the UK in the Companies Act (1985 as amended): chairman's statement, auditor's report, profit and loss statement, balance sheet and cash flow statement. The accounting rules by which they are to be constructed are prescribed in financial reporting standards (FRSs) to ensure that all companies mean the same thing when they make an entry in one of the statements. When they are completed (following the company's financial year end), they become publicly available. Each shareholder receives a copy, and a copy is lodged at UK Companies House in Cardiff or London.

It is for the purposes of comparisons of this nature that cross-sectional analyses are important. As well as comparing accounting numbers like turnover, it is often helpful to compare two or more companies' ratios (see next section), such as return on sales or one of the working capital ratios.

Ratio analysis

The third important tool in the analysis of company performance is *ratio analysis.* A ratio is a comparison (by quotient) of two items from the same set of accounts. Given that there are a lot of numbers in a set of accounts, it will not come as a surprise to learn that a large number of ratios can be drawn—some of which are more useful than others.

Ratio analysis is an area of some academic debate, and accordingly, the way in which ratios are expressed may vary between accounting and strategy textbooks. What is important therefore is to employ a consistent approach to ratio analysis, especially in longitudinal and cross-sectional analysis.

For most purposes, we can divide ratios into five broad categories:

1 Performance ratios
2 Efficiency ratios
3 Liquidity ratios
4 Investors' ratios
5 Financial structure ratios

Performance ratios

As their name suggests, performance ratios test to see how well a company has turned its inputs into profits. This usually involves comparing *return* (PBIT or profit before interest and tax) against either turnover or against its capital. This is because the rates of tax and interest payable vary. Using profit after interest and tax would distort the performance figure.

Return on capital employed (ROCE) is perhaps the most important and widely used measure of performance. It indicates the return being made compared to the funds invested. At its simplest, it is this figure that tests the gains of investing in a business as opposed to simply placing capital on return in a bank.

Where an organisation can break down its figures by divisions or subsidiaries, individual performance can be measured and decisions relating to continued ownership made.

Return on equity or *Return on ordinary shareholders' funds* gives an indication of how effectively the share capital has been turned into profit (*i.e.* it does not take account of loan capital). This ratio should be used carefully as the capital structure of the company can affect the ratio.

Return on sales, or *profit margin,* either net or gross, is a popular guide to the profitability of a company. This ratio assesses the profit made per £ (or other currency) sold. Return on sales tend's to vary from industry to industry and between companies within an industry. Airlines and tour operators, for example, typically make returns of under 10% whilst companies in the pharmaceuticals sector rarely make less than 20%. Figure 6.3 shows a graphical representation of return on sales for Air New Zealand.

Examples: Performance ratios

Each expressed as a percentage by multiplying the ratio by 100:

$$\text{Return on capital employed} = \frac{\text{PBIT (from P\&L account)}}{\text{Total capital employed}}$$

(*i.e.* one side of the balance sheet).

$$\text{Return on shareholders' funds} = \frac{\text{PBIT}}{\text{Shareholders' funds (from balance sheet)}}$$

$$\text{Net return on sales} = \frac{\text{PBIT}}{\text{Total saie (also called turnover or revenue)}}$$

$$\text{Gross return on sales} = \frac{\text{Gross profit}}{\text{Total sales}}$$

Note: Gross profit is the profit after direct costs (*i.e.* conversion cost) have been deducted from sales, but before indirect (*i.e.* administrative) costs. Gross margin is an indication of how effectively a company has managed its wages, energy and stocks.

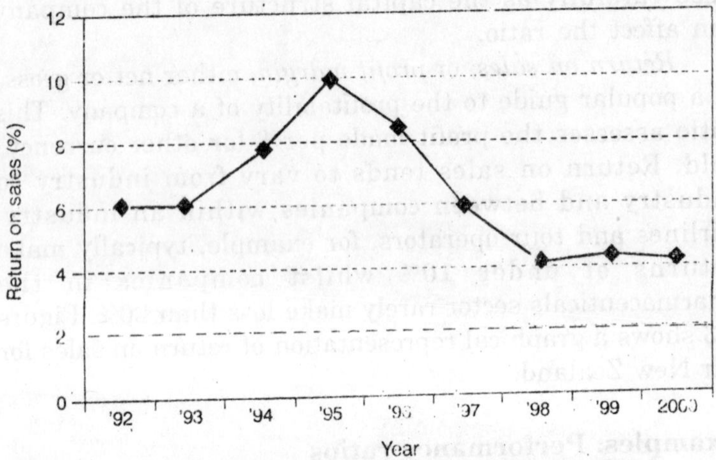

Fig. 6.3—A longitudinal analysis of Air New Zealand return on sales, 1992-2000

Efficiency ratios

These ratios show how efficiently a company has used its assets to generate sales. We can use any one of a number of a company's inputs to test against sales or profits. Common efficiency ratios include *sales per employee* and *profit per employee,* both of which test the efficiency with which a company uses its labour inputs.

Concept: Efficiency

The term efficiency is used in many ways—not just in accounting. We may speak of an efficient engine or the efficiency of a heating system in a house. At its simplest, efficiency is a comparison of a systems output to its inputs with a view to testing how well the input has been turned into output. It follows that a more efficient system will produce more output for a given input than a less efficient one.

It can be expressed mathematically as a quotient.

$$\text{Efficiency} = \frac{\text{Work output}}{\text{Work input}} \times 100 \text{ (to arrive at a percentage)}$$

Other commonly used efficiency ratios are *asset turnover* and a variant of this, *fixed asset turnover*. A high level of asset turnover indicates that the company is using its assets efficiently and, conversely, a low level may indicate that the company is suffering from overcapacity. Stock turnover gives an indication of how well the company controls its stocks. A company that keeps stock moving will generally have a higher stock turnover than one that has piles of unsaleable or obsolete materials.

Examples: Efficiency ratios

$$\text{Sales per employee (£)} = \frac{\text{Total sales (from P\&L)}}{\text{Number of employees (usually found in the notes to the accounts)}}$$

$$\text{Profit per employee (£)} = \frac{\text{PBIT}}{\text{Number of employees}}$$

$$\text{Stock turnover} = \frac{\text{Cost of sales (from P\&L)}}{\text{Value of stock (from balance sheet)}}$$

Note: Stock turnover is measured in *times—i.e.* the number of times the total stock is turned over in a given year.

Liquidity ratios

These ratios test the company's ability to meet its short-term debts—an important thing to establish if we have reason to believe the company is in trouble. Essentially, they ask the question, 'has the company enough funds to meet what it owes?'.

The *current ratio* is the best-known liquidity ratio. It is a measure of a company's total liabilities in comparison to its total assets and is thus calculated entirely from balance sheet figures. It is used to assess the company's ability to meet its liabilities by the use of its assets such as stock, debtors (receivables) and cash.

The *acid test ratio* is a variant of the current ratio and tests the company's ability to meet its short term liabilities using its cash or 'near cash' assets. Many textbooks suggest a ratio of 2:1 should be a target for this ratio and a target of 1:1 should be sought for the acid test ratio. These are simple guides and should not be taken as the norm for all industries. For example, many companies in the travel industry have low levels of stock and, as a result, their current ratio will be well below 2:1, and consequently the acid test ratio provides a better guide in such cases.

Investors' ratios

This family of ratios test for things that are important to a company's investors—usually its shareholders or potential shareholders. There are three that are widely used.

Earnings per share (EPS) are calculated by dividing profit after interest and tax (called earnings) by the number of shares. It shows how much profit is attributable to each share.

The *price earnings ratio* (P/E) gives an indication of the stockmarket's confidence in a company's shares. It is the current market price of the company's ordinary shares divided by its EPS at the last year end and it follows therefore that the P/E varies with the share price. Broadly speaking, it is a way of showing how highly investors value the earnings a company produces. A high P/E ratio (where the price is high compared to the last declared EPS) usually indicates growth potential whilst a low P/E suggests static profits. The P/E ratio for quoted companies is regularly published in the financial press.

Dividend yield is the third widely used investors' ratio. Potential shareholders often, want to know what the most recent return on the share was in terms of percentage. Dividend yield is calculated by dividing the dividend per share at the last year end by the current price (and then multiplying by 100 to arrive at a percentage).

Examples: Investors' ratios

$$\text{EPS} = \frac{\text{Profit after interest and tax}}{\text{Share volume}}$$

$$\text{P/E} = \frac{\text{Price of share (as of 'today')}}{\text{EPS at most recent year end}}$$

$$\text{Dividend yield} = \frac{\text{Gross dividend per share}}{\text{Current price of share}} \times 100$$

Financial structure ratios

We encountered financial structure above when we discussed the relative merits of loan and share capital. The way in which a company 'mixes' these forms of capital is referred to as its financial (or capital) structure.

The *gearing ratio* looks at the relationship between all the borrowings of the company (including short-term borrowings), and all the capital employed by the company. This provides a view of the extent to which borrowing forms part of the total capital base of the company and hence the risk associated with rising interest rates.

The *debt—equity ratio,* a variation on the gearing ratio, uses the shareholders' funds in the calculation rather than the total capital employed. This ratio provides a more direct comparison between the funds attributed to shareholders and liability of the company to loan providers.

Examples: Financial structure ratios

$$\text{Gearing} = \frac{\text{Debt capital (typically borrowings due after one years)}}{\text{Debt capital plus shareholders' funds}}$$

$$\text{Debt/equity ratio} = \frac{\text{Debt capital (borrowings due after one year)}}{\text{Shareholders' funds}}$$

Using ratios in financial analysis

Compared to simply looking at accounting numbers, ratios, provide a way of making some sense of published accounts. However, if we place a ratio within its longitudinal or cross-sectional context, its usefulness is maximized.

If we take return on sales as an example, we would usually want to know how Company A's figure this year compares not only with last year's (*i.e.* is it more or less), but also with Company A's competitors. This enables us to assess how Company A is performing over time and to make a judgement on its competitive position in its industry. This is because profitability is an important indicator of competitive success.

Limitations of financial information

For most purposes in strategic analysis, we can accept the proposition that the data we collect from a company's annual accounts are accurate and provide a truthful statement on its financial position. From time to time, however, we may need to qualify our analysis because of one or more reasons.

First, whilst the financial statements are audited for accuracy, other parts of the annual report are not. If our financial analysis consists of an examination of the entire document and not just the accounting sections, then we would need to be aware of this. Additional disclosures made in corporate reports may serve a number of purposes. Some commentators have suggested that such disclosures may be something of a public relations and marketing exercise.

Second, we should remember that the financial information in a corporate report is historical, often published up to three months after the period they represent. Whilst this historical information can be used to judge past performance, it may have limited use in predicting future performance. The balance sheet shows the financial position at 'a moment in time' (at the year end). It does not (unlike the P&L) summarize a full year's trading and things can sometimes change quickly after the year-end.

In an attempt to avoid this potential problem, Stock Exchange quoted companies are required to produce interim reports, normally half yearly and unaudited, which show their profit and turnover for that period. Quoted companies are also required to provide the Stock Exchange with information that may have a significant impact on its prospects such as changes on the Board or anything that gives rise to a 'profits warning'.

Third, those who prepare a company's financial statements (the financial accountants) sometimes have cause to 'hide' bad news so as to avoid alarming the company's investors. It is possible to employ legal financial restructuring so as to make some figures appear better than perhaps they are. A year on year increase in the value of fixed assets, for example, may appear at first glance to be healthy, but it may be that the company has accumulated a high amount of debt to finance it. It is for this reason that we sometimes need to examine all parts of a company's financial statements to spot any countervailing bad news that has been obscured by the company in its reporting.

Finance and risk in travel and tourism

Foreign exchange risk analysis

The travel and tourism industry operates internationally, producing international flows of funds in various currencies. Tour operators and airlines, for example, typically have a very large exposure to movements in foreign exchange rates, almost certainly far larger than for most companies of a similar size engaged in other areas of the economy (manufacturing companies, for example). The very purpose of these companies implies that they are international in their activities, thereby leaving them exposed to international risks associated with foreign exchange transactions.

The profitability of any company that trades internationally is affected by changes in foreign exchange rates. As Lockwood (1989) stated: 'as a large part of the travel and tourist industry is concerned with persuading and assisting people to cross national boundaries and thus to buy goods and services priced in a foreign currency, the identification and management of exchange rate exposures is vital to the profitable operation of a travel and tourist business'.

Thus foreign exchange management is very significant for many travel and tourism businesses. The lack of stability caused by the continual changes in exchange rates between currencies creates uncertainty. Specifically, uncertainty is created as to:

- what foreign income will be worth when it is received;
- what payments will cost when they have to be made;
- what the value of foreign assets and liabilities might be in the future.

British Airways' foreign exchange exposure

The overall foreign exchange position of a company may be complicated as illustrated by the position of British Airways: 'The group does business in approximately 140 foreign currencies which account for approximately 60% of Group Revenue and approximately 40% of operating expenses. The Group generates a surplus in most of these currencies [*i.e.* revenues are greater than costs]. The principal exceptions are the US dollar and the pound sterling in which the Group has a deficit arising from capital expenditure and the payment of some leasing costs, together with expenditure on fuel, which is payable in US dollars and the majority of staff costs, central overheads and other leasing costs, which are payable in pounds sterling'.

Source: British Airways Annual Report and Accounts, 1998-99.

It is imperative to the profitability of many companies operating in the travel and tourism industry that this exposure to foreign exchange rate movements is recognised and managed appropriately.

In all cases risk attributed to foreign exchange rate movements arises out of uncertainty about the future exchange rate between two currencies. This risk would be minimised if it were possible to predict future rate movements. Unfortunately, it is not possible to do so with any degree of accuracy, and for a company to try to do so can be financially dangerous. If foreign exchange rates cannot be predicted, another option might be to pass on to the customer the effects of any adverse movements in exchange rates, and hence the company would incur to impact. In most cases, however, the highly competitive nature of the travel and tourism business prevents higher costs being passed on to the customer in this way. Clearly then it is prudent to manage these risks, although it is common in the industry for the risks to be ignored, especially by smaller companies.

Types of risk exposure

We can identify three different types of foreign exchange risk or exposure a company may be faced with:

Transaction exposure

Transaction exposure arises, 'because the cost or proceeds (in home currency) of settlement of a future payment or receipt denominated in another currency may vary due to changes in exchange rates' (Buckley, 2000).

Transaction exposure relates to the foreign exchange exposure where contracts have already been entered into. When a company has contracted to receive or pay an amount of money in a foreign currency at some time in the future a risk is incurred. The specific risk is that adverse exchange rate movements between now and the time of the eventual cash receipt/payment will increase the amount to be paid out or decrease the amount to be received.

For example, a UK tour operator selling holidays to America would receive its income in pounds sterling but have to make payments to hoteliers and other suppliers in US dollars. In order to make the payments at some stage the company would have to convert sterling into US dollars. This would entail a risk that the US dollar might rise in value (appreciate) against sterling, thereby making the payments more expensive in sterling terms. Assume, for instance, the company had costed its hotel beds in its American programme at a rate of $1.50 to the pound (*i.e.* 1 pound buys 1.50 US dollars), and that the total cost to purchase the required bed spaces was $1500 000. The cost in sterling to the company would be $1500 000/1.50 = £1 000 000. Now if the rate subsequently fell to $1.40 the cost would increase to $1500 000/1.40 = £1071429.

Translation exposure

As Buckley (2000) states, 'Translation exposure arises on the consolidation of assets, liabilities and profits, denominated in foreign currency in the process of preparing consolidated accounts'.

The concept is also known as *accounting exposure.* For example, if a UK hotel company purchases a hotel in Australia, it acquires an asset priced in Australian dollars. Each year when the balance sheet of the business is prepared, the value of the hotel would be translated into sterling at the prevailing rate on the balance sheet date. The hotel might therefore be worth less in sterling terms as shown in the balance sheet of the company.

Economic exposure

Economic exposure (sometimes referred to as political exposure) arises from the effect of adverse exchange rate movements on future cash flows, where no contractual arrangement to receive or pay money has yet been made. This kind of exposure is longer term in nature and often difficult to quantify exactly and forecast accurately.

For instance, suppose a specialist tour operator operates most of its programme to one country, perhaps Gambia for example. The company will have a high economic exposure to that country and its currency. In some countries the political and economic circumstances are very uncertain, and if, for example, the government should be replaced in a violent way, (as occurred in recent years in Gambia), customers will be reluctant to book holidays to that country, thereby severely limiting the revenues of the specialist tour operator.

Thus, movements in foreign exchange rates lead to a number of different problems or exposures for travel and tourism companies. These exposures can be dealt with in a number of ways. The most obvious ways of dealing with such exposures are to avoid the exposures altogether, either by trading in domestic markets only, or by passing the exposure over to suppliers or customers. These alternatives are seldom possible in international travel and tourism, so other management methods such as the use of forward foreign exchange contracts or foreign exchange options have to be employed in order to reduce the risks. For a full discussion of these methods see Samuel, Wilkes and Brayshaw (1995) and Ross (1996).

Cash flow risk analysis

Travel and tourism has one of the most highly seasonal patterns of demand for any product, with less variation than the demand for Christmas cards or air conditioners, but more than nearly all high value individual purchases (Bull, 1995). This seasonality is largely due to climate, but is also related to factors such as school holidays, festivals and historic travel patterns. Seasonality of demand for the product leads to a highly seasonal pattern of cash inflows and outflows. Consequently, at certain times of the year companies may have large cash balances to invest and at other times of the year many companies need to borrow money in order to maintain payments to suppliers (creditors). The industry is also *cyclical* in nature, in that cash flows are very responsive to changes in the general level of economic activity.

In terms of cash management, tour operators, travel agents and airlines are typically low margin businesses, deriving important parts of their income, not from operating profits (through the selling of travel arrangements), but from interest income derived from investing cash surpluses they may be holding at certain times of the year.

Seasonality of cash flow for a UK tour operator

If we take as an example a typical UK outbound tour operator selling mass-market package holidays largely to Europe, it is greatly affected by the seasonality of the product and this directly affects its cash flow and in turn its management.

Such an operator may have a number of operating characteristics:

- the bulk of holidays sold would be summer sun, with the season lasting from April to September, but with the peak months being July and August during school holidays.
- Summer sun holidays are typically booked in three distinct periods:
  - (i) The *early booking period starting in August or September,* when a significant number of people book. This applies especially to families, and those who are tied to taking holidays between certain dates, or are trying to take advantage of particular offers such as 'free child places', or low deposits.
  - (ii) *The post Christmas period from January to March,* which is usually the largest booking period, and during which customers may be targeted with a second edition of the brochure.
  - (iii) *The late booking period, from April onwards,* which has become increasingly significant in recent years, and may be a time of intense competition as operators try to sell remaining capacity and vary prices in order to do so.
- Many tour operators have attempted to widen their range of activities, and reduce the effects of seasonality, by, for instance, introducing winter sun and skiing programmes. The winter sun season normally lasts from October to April, whilst the skiing season normally lasts from December to April with peaks in February and at Easter. In most cases the combined size of these programmes is far

smaller than the summer programme, representing perhaps 25% of the summer programme in terms of receipts. Bookings for the winter sun and skiing programmes are taken throughout the summer and autumn, but the winter ski programme in particular is subject to a great deal of late booking in late autumn and early winter as customers wait to see what snow conditions are likely for the season.

- The tour operator will have a number of seasonal costs such as airline fuel, staff working at resorts, and accommodation charges. However, the tour operator will also have a high level of costs that have to be met throughout the year, such as the costs of head office staff aircraft maintenance and computer facilities.

The characteristics of the tour operating business outlined in the box entitled 'Seasonality of cash flow for a UK tour operator' have certain implications for cash flow analysis and cash management. Cash builds up and declines in a seasonal way. During certain times of the year, particularly in the spring, large surplus cash balances are free to be invested until the cash is needed to pay bills during the summer season and for the remainder of the year. The size and timing of the cash balances, and the interest to be earned from the invested balances will vary from year to year, since the profile of bookings and level of interest rates also vary from year to year.

The period of greatest risk for many travel and tourism companies, however, usually comes in the autumn and winter. Cash balances have been run down as seasonal payments have been made during the preceding summer season and the bulk of bookings for the subsequent season have yet to be made. The position is often exacerbated by companies offering favourable payment terms to customers whereby a low initial deposit is required. Companies often have to rely on bank support to help them through this period.

The problems of cash flow may be compounded, however, if the early summer booking period for the forthcoming season and winter ski and sun bookings are poor, and post Christmas bookings are delayed.

In a case where a bank (or other party) fails to lend the necessary support, insolvency is the inevitable result. Insolvency (the inability to pay bills as they become due), has often befallen companies in this sector when revenue from expected bookings has failed to materialise.

When a company reaches an insolvent position it normally leads to the company's failure and liquidation. A company can sometimes survive for many years without making profits or making very low levels of profit, but if they run out of cash it is difficult for them to survive, because employees and creditors must be paid. Many travel and tourism companies routinely rely on banks to provide short-term finance for a part of the year, but it is when these negative cash balances are larger or more prolonged than usual and banks feel unable to provide finance that problems occur.

Fig. 6.4 illustrates the cash flow problems described above for Interjet, a fictional small outbound UK tour operator with ambitious plans. The company plans to increase its sales turnover by around 25% each year. However, like many tour operators, travel agents and other tourism businesses, the company experiences annual seasonal cash flow difficulties. A cash flow forecast has been prepared for the following financial years and this is shown in Fig. 6.4.

On analysing the cash flow, the following may be necessary:

- Insert all known income and payments for each period on to a cash flow schedule (as illustrated in the case of Interjet, Fig. 6.4)
- Income and payments should be totalled to produce a balance carried forward to next period.
- Forecast future cash flow using available information.

	1 Apr.	2 May	3 June	4 July	5 Aug.	6 Sept.	7 Oct.	8 Nov.	9 Dec.	10 Jan.	11 Feb.	12 Mar.	Total
Inflows													
Receipts from debtors	230	250	120	50	60	75	80	90	110	150	220	320	1744
Dividend on investment							45						
Total inflows	230	250	120	50	60	75	125	90	110	150	220	320	1800
Outflows													
Payment to creditors		80		80		88		88		88		92	516
Wages and others expenses	102	77	58	103	79	59	105	80	62	108	83	63	979
Payments for fixed assests				80	10	15					5		100
Dividend payable			80										80
Corporation tax									120				120
Total outflows	102	157	138	253	89	162	105	168	182	196	88	155	1795
Net in/out	128	93	–18	–203	–29	–87	20	–78	–72	–46	132	165	5
Bank balance													
Opening	30	158	251	233	30	1	–86	–66	–144	–216	–262	–130	
Closing	158	251	233	30	1	–86	–6	–144	–216	–262	–130	35	

Notes:

a. As a tour operator, most funds are received by customers as a deposit and subsequent payment of balance. On average this results in 3 months' credit being granted to customers.

b. On average 6 weeks' credit is taken from customers.

c. Capital expenditure budget:

New computer facilities	Month 4	40000
Routine replacement of motor vehicles.	Month 4	30000
Computer software and programming costs.	Month 5	10000
Progress payment on building extensions.	Month 7~	15000
Office furniture and equipment.	Month 11	5000

d. Negotiated overdraft facilities currently stand at 60000.

Fig. 6.4. Interjet - cash flow forecast (£000s)

- Produce 'sensitivity' analyses, *i.e.* what if, for instance sales were 10% lower/higher than expected or jet fuel prices rose by 50%?
- Produce a graph showing monthly or weekly balances may help indicate trends.

Analysis of the cash flow should prompt certain questions such as:

- How easily predictable are the cash flows?
- How seasonal or cyclical are the cash flows?
- Can the company keep within its borrowing limits?
- Is the company generating enough cash to ensure its survival?
- Does the company require further credit facilities?
- How long does it take customers to pay the company?
- How quickly does the company pay suppliers and others?

There are a number of actions a company may wish to consider to alleviate perceived cash flow problems including:

- Postponing capital expenditure.
- Accelerating cash inflows.
- Postponing or reducing cash outflows.
- Selling assets.
- Negotiating new lines of credit.
- Leasing rather than buying equipment.

7

The Adventure Tourism Industry

Introduction

Adventure tourism is a complex industry with a wide variety of elements and suppliers. Some of these suppliers are also part of the mainstream tourism industry, such as accommodation operators, while others are specific to adventure tourism, like equipment manufacturers. The structure of the adventure tourism industry is illustrated in Figure 7.1.

It is also possible, as we will now see, to look at the structure of the industry in several other ways.

The structure of the industry

A wide range of suppliers meet the demand for adventure tourism, and these can be looked at in different ways as in Figure 7.1.

Clearly this is a gross over-simplification. For example:

1. Some types of suppliers, such as equipment suppliers and tour operators, can be found in both the generation zone and the destination zone.
2. Some types of suppliers can be sub-divided into many different categories.

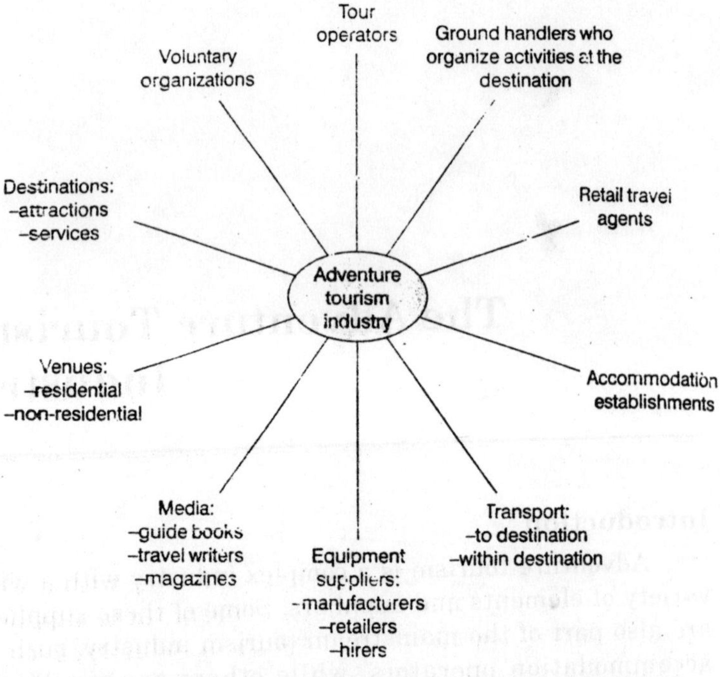

Fig. 7.1—The structure of the adventure tourism industry.

For example, accommodation for adventure tourists could encompass:

- Sleeping in the open in the wilderness where no permission is required, no equipment is needed and no fee is paid for the accommodation.
- Camping in the wilderness, which is free and camping on owned land where a fee is payable.
- Building a shelter in the wilderness or on owned land where a 'rental price' for the land may or may not be payable.
- Making use of existing buildings or shelters that are either derelict or are usually used for a different purpose.
- Using accommodation that has been tailor-made for adventure tourists, such as mountain refuge huts.

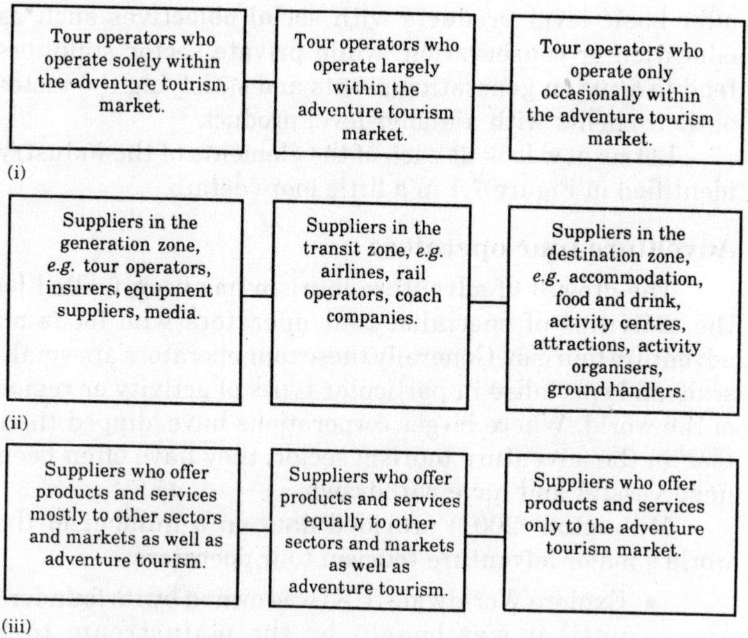

Fig. 7.2—Three dimensions of the supply side of adventure tourism.

- Combined transport and accommodation, such as long-distance sailing races where competitors sleep on board their boat.
- Novel indigenous forms of accommodation, such as rorbus, yurts and ice caves.
- Shared use of destination accommodation that is also used by other leisure and/or business tourists.
- The use of both serviced and self-catering accommodation.
- The use of luxury accommodation so that the adventure is a daytime activity only, while the nights mean pampering, warmth and safety.

Figure 7.2 has clearly not distinguished between suppliers who are in the private, public and voluntary sectors. As we will see in the chapter on marketing, this distinction has a great influence on the nature of products, pricing levels, and promotional messages. Public and voluntary bodies often offer basic level products with social objectives such as education or conservation, while private sector suppliers tend to focus on generating profits and satisfying the tastes of their clients with a higher-level product.

Let us now look at each of the elements of the industry identified in Figure 7.1 in a little more detail.

Adventure tour operators

The growth of adventure tourism has been fuelled by the activities of specialist tour operators who focus on adventure tourism. Generally these tour operators are small-scale and specialise in particular types of activity or region of the world. Where larger corporations have 'dipped their toes' in the adventure tourism sector, they have often been unsuccessful and have withdrawn.

Millington (2001) provided data on a number of the world's major adventure tourism tour operators:

- Explore Worldwide (UK) was owned by its founders until it was bought by the mainstream tour operator, the Holidaybreak Group, in 2000. In 2001 the operator sold around 22000 packages, and made £1.3 million profit between September 2000 and March 2001. Explore offers a wide range of activities in many different regions of the world.
- Exodus (UK) is a close competitor of Explore Worldwide, and carries around 12000 passengers a year. The company started in 1974 with tours to Afghanistan, a destination that was very trendy with young travellers in the 1970s.
- Dragoman (UK) has been in business for a quarter of a century and has a strong reputation for working with local communities.
- Abercrombie and Kent (UK) was founded in 1962, and is renowned for offering packages at the luxury end of the adventure travel market. Therefore many of its packages are not true 'adventure experiences' and only a proportion of its 180000 clients per year can be truly seen as adventure tourists. A new

offshoot, A & K Active, focuses more on activity holidays than the traditional Abercrombie and Kent vacation, which tends to be more about sightseeing.

- Trek America (USA), which is now 30 years old, focuses on selling adventure packages in the USA, Canada and Mexico to Americans and foreigners. Its on-line brochure site enjoys around 4 million hits per annum.
- Lindblad Travel (USA) has been around since 1958, and concentrates on taking Americans for adventures on other continents. Now it even owns its own ships for adventure cruising.
- Mountain Travel Sobek (USA) is a result of a merger in 1991 between Mountain Travel (mountain expedition specialists) and Sobek (a river-rafting company). Since this merger, the company has sought to boost its market appeal.
- Geographic Expeditions (USA), set up in 1983, concentrates on small-scale special interest vacations to adventurous destinations and has around 4500 clients every year.
- Canadian Mountain Holidays (Canada) concentrates on vacations to very remote, little visited places, but with an emphasis on luxury. The company was founded in 1979 and carries about 4000 passengers each year. It claims to have invented heli-sking and now has a range of products aimed at families.
- Wikinger Reisen (Germany) is more than 30 years old and now services some 16000 clients per annum and employs 200 staff.
- DAV Summit Club (Germany) focuses on walking and climbing holidays all over the world.
- Terres d'Adventure (France) carries around 17000 passengers per annum and focuses on solo adventure and family adventure.
- Explorator (France) focuses on four-wheel drive vehicle tours and services around 4000 (generally high income) clients each year.

This survey illustrates the diversity of tour operators in adventure tourism, but they all share the characteristic that they are small, niche-market operators. They are therefore quite weak in relation to larger operators, and hence it is not surprising that many small operators are forming strategic alliances to give them more power in the marketplace. For example, Exodus in the UK has teamed up with Peregrine Adventures and Geckos to form 'This Amazing Planet', which focuses on environmentally responsible tourism. Each company has different target markets, but they are involved in joint marketing activities.

Most adventure trips are not 'hard' vacations but are relatively 'soft', in small groups. Two examples are given here from the UK-based company Sundowners' 2001 brochure.

Karakoram & Kashgar

21 Days, £1960 Twin Share

Pakistan and China

From the North West Frontier Province to the great mountain regions of northern Pakistan, the Hindu Kush, Karakoram and Pamir ranges collide to produce some of the world's most breathtaking scenery.

Hidden valleys and high passes lead the way through Chirtal, Chiligit and Hunza to the Khunjerab pass and China's Xinjian province. This was the way of the silk caravans on their journey from Xian to Kashmir and in more recent history the lands where the rivalries for territory between Britain and Russia became known as the 'Great Game'. To travel this region independently is to follow in the footsteps of Silk Road merchants, spies, geographers and eccentrics who were the pioneers of travel to this incredible land. A truly remarkable travel experience.

Itinerary Guideline

Day 1 Islamabad

Pakistan's capital is a modern planned city

Day 2 Taxila to Peshawar

Visit the ruined city of Taxila *en route* to the frontier town of Peshawar.

Day 3 Peshawar

The bazzar reflects Peshawar's location as gateway to the Khyber Pass; opium and hashish, arms and ammunitions view for space alongside carpets and spices, food and clothing.

Days 4-6 North West Frontier Province

North to the Swat valley, over the Lowari Pass (3118 m) to Chitral and visit the Kafir people of the Kalash valleys.

Days 7-9 to Gillgit

Through the spectacular Hindu Raj mountains and over the Shandur Pass (3734m) to Gilgit.

Days 10-12 To Hunza

Walk in the Hunza valley with magnificent views of Rakaposhi (7788m) and the surrounding peaks and glaciers before continuing to Sust.

Days 13 & 14 Khunjerab Pass to Kashgar

Over the Khunjerab Pass (4730m) to China and the old fortress town of Tashkurgan and on to the legendary Silk Road market town of Kashgar.

Days 15 & 16 Kashgar

The Sunday market is not to be missed as Uighar, Tadjik and Kyrgyz gather to buy, sell and exchange in an age-old tradition.

Days 17 & 18 Across the Karakoram

Return to Pakistan and the Hunza valley

Day 19-21 Karakoram highway

Down the Karakoram highway via Chilas and Besham to Islamabad

Details

Commences—Daily from Islamabad [Saturday recommended]

Travel by—Four-wheel drive jeep, local and chartered vehicle

Stay in—Hotels and guesthouses 18 nights, camping 2 nights

Meals—Included when camping from lunch day 7 to lunch day 9

Grade—**Adventurous**

Notes—Some hard travelling and high passes—expect an outstanding adventure. Travelling season May to October.

Supplements for single travellers £1440

Dossier—Available on request.

In the Footsteps of Alexander

26 Days, £1990

Conquer Asia on this truly epic journey. Fellow in the footsteps of Alexander the Great and Marco Polo from the fertile Indus Valley, cradle of civilisation, across the vast and inhospitable deserts of Central Asia, through ancient

Persia to the Bosphorous—gateway to Europe. Between lies a world of lost civilisations, amazing architecture and mysterious and fascinating people.

History unfolds as you follow this ancient route of trade and conquest, revealing the rise and fall of monumental empires and the legendary heroes, ancient and modern, who ventured into this land of fable suspended between East and West.

Your Itinerary

Days 1 & 2—Arrive Lahore. Enjoy a full day sightseeing, including Badshahi mosque. Lahore Fort, Shalimar gardens and the old city. *3*—Drive to Multan, known as the 'city of saints', via one of the Indus valley's most important ancient cities, Harappa. Explore the fascinating ruins dating from 3500 BC. *4*—A morning tour of Multan includes the Shah Tukne-Alam tomb and Agahi bazzar, one of the most colourful in Pakistan and full of pottery and handicrafts. Then to Uchh, famous for the beautiful tombs of the Sufi saints. Then to Bahawalpur. *5*—Drive to Sukkur on the banks of the Indus river. *6 & 7*—Morning boat ride on the Indus before departing for the ruins of Mohenjodaro, one of the Indus valley's earliest civilisations. Then through the spectacular Bolan pass to Quetta. *8 & 9*—Across the remote Baluchiastan desert to Iran. *10*—To Bam, where we explore the beautifully preserved citadel. *11*—To Kerman, carpet capital of the world. *12 & 13*—To the cultural centre of ancient Persia, Shiraz. We visit the massive stone ruins of Darius the Great's Persepolis. *14 & 15*—To the majestic city of Isfahan, with the greatest concentration of Islamic monuments in the country. *16 & 17*—To the capital Tehrań and on to Tabriz. *18 & 19*—To Turkey, passing Mt Ararat, fabled resting place of Noah's Ark. Visit the spectacular Isak Pasa Sarayi fortress before heading across eastern Anatolia to Erzurum. *20-23*—North to the Black Sea with time to explore the quaint coastal towns and beaches before driving to the capital Ankara. *24-26*—To Istanbul, Turkey's most exciting and interesting city. Visit the infamous Blue Mosque and old town before our epic journey concludes at this meeting point of East and West.

Details

Escorted—Maximum Group size: 15

Travel by—Chartered and local vehicles, some sightseeing by foot and boat.

Stay in—Budget hotels/guesthouses.
Meals—Not included.
You will experience—An epic journey that links Asia with Europe, revealing the rich cultures and history of Pakistan, Iran and Turkey little seen by the western traveller.
Grade—Adventurous.
Notes—Although this journey is scheduled in the most favourable season, temperatures can still be high during the day and it can be cold overnight, particularly in the desert regions. The distance covered should not be under-estimated—there are some long travelling days. Combines with 'Oases of the Silk Road'.
Dossier—Available on request.

Adventure ground handlers

Tour operators are the companies in the country from which the tourist travels, which organise the whole package. Within destination, there are ground handlers. These are the companies that organise activities within the destination, either on behalf of the tour operators or for independent travellers. These ground handlers usually specialise in particular activities. They are important because they determine the quality of the adventure experience, as they are the actual people who offer the activities to the tourists on a face-to-face basis. Some idea of the nature and scope of ground handlers is illustrated in the following examples:

- Salty's in Bundaberg (Queensland), a company that runs diving trips on the Great Barrier Reef
- Gecko Canoe Tours, which offers three-to-six-day canal trips from Kalterine in the Nitmiluh National Park
- Impacto Turismo, which runs eco-tours in the Pantanal wetlands region of Brazil
- Amazon's Indian Turismo, which is run by Amazonian Indians and offers basic jungle-trekking and wildlife trips in Brazilian Amazonia
- Svalbard Polar Travel of Norway, which offers a five-day adventure cruise around Svalbard involving landings in isolated locations

- Idide Ride Sled Dog Tours, which offers short day sled tours in the Kenai Peninsular of Alaska
- Tion Shan Travel in Bishbek, which offers heli-skiing trips, as well as trekking, in the mountains of Kyrgyzstan
- Small plane sightseeing tours of glaciers on Alaska, at $90-$140 dollars per person, offered by several local ground handlers.

The ground handlers play a vital role in adventure travel in that, as the organizers of the adventure activities, they are primarily responsible for the safety of travellers.

Travel agents

Most adventure tourism tour operators sell their products directly to clients without the need for intermediaries. However, several travel agencies specialise in selling adventure packages or making travel arrangements for individual adventure travellers and backpackers.

Trailfinders (UK), for example, was founded in 1970 and now makes travel arrangements for around 800 000 people per annum. It accounts for 20 per cent of all British leisure travellers to Australia. The company also works with specialist tour operators such as Exodus. Trek America, Journey Latin America. Guerba, Dragoman Encounter, Contiki, and the Imaginative Traveller (Millington, 2001).

Equipment suppliers

Much adventure tourism is based on activities that require specialist equipment. This in turn creates a need for equipment manufacturers, retailers and hire companies. Some of this equipment (such as micro-light aircraft) costs thousands of pounds, while other items cost just a few pounds. Equipment includes the hardware people need to undertake an activity as well as the specialist clothing required to take part in the activity. Major considerations in relation to the purchase of equipment include safety and fashionability.

Manufacturers and retailers of equipment and clothing advertise heavily in the adventure travel magazines. The range of equipment suppliers involved in adventure tourism is illustrated by the contents of a randomly selected issue of *Adventure Travel Outdoors* magazine from 2001. This magazine contained the following:

- Fifteen advertisements for equipment manufacturers
- Twenty-four advertisements for equipment retailers
- Seven advertisements for specialist clothing
- Thirteen reviews of new pieces of equipment
- Eight advertisements for services offered to adventure tourists.

The scope of equipment in adventure tourism is shown by the following selection of types of equipment, clothing or service advertised in the same issue of *Adventure Travel Outdoors:*

- Blister cream
- Duvets
- Expedition packs
- Guidebooks
- Food
- Gaiters
- Insect repellent
- Insurance
- Knives
- Rucksacks
- Torches
- Watches
- Waterproof clothing
- Maps
- Tents

Equipment manufacturing and retailing tends to take place in the tourists' home country. However, many adventure travellers rely on hiring equipment and clothing in their destinations. This is particularly the case where:

- Tourists decide to take part in activities that they did not envisage participating in when they planned their vacation
- Tourists participate in a new activity while on vacation
- The cost of transporting the tourists' own gear and clothing is prohibitive

- Local conditions demand specialist equipment that is designed specifically for the locality.

Some idea of rental charges is given in the following examples taken from the USA in 2000 (prices are in US dollars):

- Bike hire in Alaska—$20 per day
- Kayak rental in Alaska—$50 per day for a single
- Cross-country skis—$20 per day
- Wetsuits and surfboards—$30 per day
- Bear-resistant food containers, in national parks—free from the park authorities.

Accommodation

Adventure tourists require sleeping accommodation, but often it is very different from that used by mainstream tourists. The most popular forms of accommodation for adventure tourists are :

- Sleeping rough, in the open
- Camping
- Youth and other hostels
- Mountain huts and refuges.

Much of this accommodation is either free or is offered at very low cost by non-profit-making organisations.

Some adventure tourists like to stay with local people, in everything from longhouses in Borneo to bed-and-breakfast in Alaska. Here the price paid is a 'commercial' rate, but it is paid to private individual or families and not to commercial operations.

Often the form of accommodation is part of the actual adventure experience, but sometimes the accommodation is the core of the adventure. This category may include ice-hotels or igloos in the Arctic North of Scandinavia and North America, or the 'tree hotels' in several jungle regions of the world.

At the higher end of the adventure market there are those who want to sleep in luxurious or at least comfortable accommodation, and then be transported to the adventure each day.

Transport

The transport needs of adventure tourists are of two kinds: first to the destination, and then within the destination. Because of the remoteness of many adventure tourism destinations, travel to them is often a complex process involving several flights, bus journeys or slow train journeys.

Furthermore, the riskiness of the journey to the destination can be part of the adventure itself, providing stories for the traveller to recount in the years to come. These risks can involve old aircraft, bad weather, dangerous terrain, or the threat of terrorist action.

Once at the destination a wide variety of modes of transport are utilised including:

- Walking
- Cross-country skiing
- Aircraft and helicopters
- Cycling
- Horse, camel and donkey riding
- Hire cars
- Commercial lorries
- Buses and coaches
- Trains
- Canoes, boats and ferries.

One particular way of travelling is hitching—a way of moving around that is an adventure in itself. There are risks of being attacked or of simply not getting a lift. Hitching is viewed as a particularly adventurous or risky activity for lone women travellers.

Finally, sometimes the act of travelling is in itself the adventure. This is true of great rail journeys such as the Trans-Siberian Express or the Orient Express, together with seaplane flights and trips on ice-breaking slips.

Media

The adventure tourism media consist of four major elements:

1. *Guide books.* Adventure tourists have had an increasingly large choice of guide books in recent years to help them plan their activities. Some focus on particular types of activity, such as skiing or wildlife watching, but the most popular and influential guide books are those produced for whole countries—such as those published by Lonely Planet, Let's Go, and Rough Guide. These books particularly influence the growing market of independent adventure travellers and backpackers. Their influence is reinforced by the websites they offer. These books and websites are often the only major source of information about a country for a traveller, so they have a great responsibility in terms of where tourists go and how they will behave.
2. *Travel writing.* Travel writing, particularly in relation to adventure tourism has boomed in recent years and now takes up many shelves in large bookshops around the world. Traditionally such writing focused on expeditions to remote and dangerous places. Today, however, adventure travel writing covers a wider variety of tourism experiences, notably:
   - The explorations of solo female travellers like Dervla Murphy
   - Visits to war zones and areas where there is a major terrorist threat
   - The travels of disabled people
   - Personal spiritual or emotional travel experiences
   - Sexual and romantic adventures while on vacation

Later in the book the reader will find a short case study which focuses specifically on adventure travel writing.

3. *Specialist magazines.* Specialist adventure travel magazines have grown in number dramatically in recent years, particularly in the so-called developed world. Some focus on particular adventures, such

as gliding or mountaineering, while others focus on destinations. Such magazines are a key influence on the positive decisions of adventure travellers in terms of both destinations and equipment. A case study of two UK-based adventure travel magazines is to be found later in this book.

4. *Television adventure travel programmes.* Television—terrestrial and satellite—has taken to adventure travel and has realised that it makes attractive television. If an adventure activity or destination is featured in a television programme, it will stimulate demand. Television has also started to play a role in organising some experiments in adventure travel—for example, in 2000 a production company produced a top-rating show based on putting a selection of ordinary people on an isolated Scottish island as 'castaways'. Likewise, many programmes are now being made about ordinary people being sent into the wilderness with the aim of adapting to their surroundings and 'surviving'.

All of the media outlined here share responsibility for the results of their activities, which may cause problems in terms of achieving sustainable adventure tourism by:

- Raising the profile of, and stimulating people's desire to visit, fragile, remote environments
- Encouraging behaviour that is not sensitive to the environment or host community, *e.g.* scuba diving
- Photography and four-wheel driving
- Failing to give travellers information to allow them to be sensitive tourists.

Voluntary organisations

Most of the adventure tourism industry is commercial and is profit-oriented. However, the voluntary sector plays a significant role in the industry in several ways; for example:

- There are activity centres and mountain holidays and refuges that are run by voluntary, non profit-making bodies

- Professional bodies that are wholly or largely voluntary sector, such as the British Mountaineering Council, often regulate adventure activities and/or develop codes of conduct for participants
- It provides voluntary labour such as instructors and group leaders.

Venues

While most adventure tourism is outdoors based, some of it is based in or on venues. This subject is dealt with in further detail in Chapter, but venues include:

- Outdoor activity centres
- Facilities such as gliding and flying clubs and diving centres
- Artificial climbing walls.

New venues can help put places on the map as adventure tourism destinations.

Destinations

Destinations for adventure tourism are discussed in detail in Chapter. Suffice it to say at this stage that destinations are crucial to adventure tourism. Sometimes the destination is the core of the experience because of its landscape or climate, while at other times it is an incidental background to the activities. In any event, it is the place where tourists enjoy their adventure tourism experience.

It is now an appropriate time for us to look at the nature of entrepreneurship in adventure tourism—a sector where the small business dominates.

Entrepreneurship in adventure tourism

Adventure tourism, as we have seen, is an 'industry' dominated by small and medium-sized enterprises and the entrepreneurial flair of individuals.

Any study of businesses in the sector reveals the existence of a certain type of enterprise, as shown in Figure 7.3.

A person enjoys a particular activity or type of holiday, such as trekking

To allow the person to maximize the time spent on this activity or type of holiday, he or she sets up a part-time 'hobby' enterprise that is combined with a full-time job. This may involve leading several treks a year during holidays from work, for example

The enterprise grows and the person finds it difficult to combine the enterprise with a full-time job

The person suddenly, or slowly over time, replaces the full-time job with work for the enterprise

In the early stages, when business for the enterprise falls temporarily, the person may supplement his or her income with part-time employment

Once the enterprise is established, it needs to expand and take on extra staff

If the enterprise grows too much, the person may feel that he or she is losing control and/or is not enjoying work as much because there is less contact with clients.

The person may therefore endeavour artificially to contain the growth of the enterprise

If the enterprise grows too large for the taste of the person, he or she may sell the enterprise and go off to start a new enterprise

Fig. 7.3—The evolution of small enterprises in adventure tourism.

Of course many enterprises do not follow this pattern, for they never become established and fail. However, enterprises like those described in Figure 7.3 can be seen throughout adventure tourism.

These enterprises also give lie to the capitalist theory that entrepreneurs will always seek to maximize profits. Many entrepreneurs in this sector clearly do not try to make as much money as possible, but instead endeavour to achieve a high quality, balanced lifestyle that provides enough money to allow them and their families to live comfortably while giving them enough free time to enjoy leisure activities or time with their family. This approach to entrepreneurship seems to be growing in popularity in today's world and adventure tourism offers some excellent real world examples.

Clearly this phenomenon is not unique to adventure tourism: it is also being seen elsewhere, such as in the small hotel sector and in other industries such as information technology.

An interesting final point is that the very act of setting up a new enterprise, of becoming an entrepreneur, is in itself an adventure—a step into the unknown!

The non-physical adventure sector

Understandably we have focused on physical adventure, which is the heart of the adventure tourism industry. However, spiritual, intellectual and emotional adventure tourism have their own infrastructure or suppliers—for example:

- Spiritual adventures—monasteries and religious retreat communities
- Gambling—casinos
- Hedonism—night clubs.

At the same time they also make use of transport and have their own specialist media.

Human resources in adventure tourism

Adventure tourism is a service industry where the human resources that staff the industry are of great importance. The safety and enjoyment of adventure tourists is often dependent on the quality of people such as tour leaders, guides and instructors. There are many technical qualifications and professional bodies that regulate the quality of such staff, but there is still a lack of formal education and training for those involved in the management of adventure tourism.

Volunteers also play a significant role in staffing the adventure tourism industry. It is, of course, more difficult to manage and control the activities of volunteers, but they are an indispensible resource for many adventure tourism organisations.

8

Marketing

Introduction

The complexity of adventure tourism as a phenomenon, which we have noted throughout the book, is reflected in the nature of marketing within the sector. Some of the intricacies of adventure tourism marketing are identified in Fig. 8.1 and we will look at each of these in a little detail.

Complexities of marketing

1. *The producers and suppliers of adventure tourism products and experiences have a variety of different objectives.* These affect their approach to marketing. For many companies, adventure tourism is a business from which they want to make a healthy profit. At the other extreme there are voluntary or non-profit-making organisations offering adventure tourism experiences, where the aim is largely social. This could include those who run 'charity challenges', or 'character building', 'horizon-widening' holidays for disadvantaged children. In between there are those adventure tourism enthusiasts who set up enterprises that allow them to pursue their former 'hobby' as a full-time profession. They often do not see profit maximization as their aim, but rather seek to balance an enjoyable lifestyle with earning enough income to enjoy a reasonable standard of living. These differences in objectives will be reflected in the approach taken

to promotion in terms of how much is done and the nature of the messages transmitted about the product.

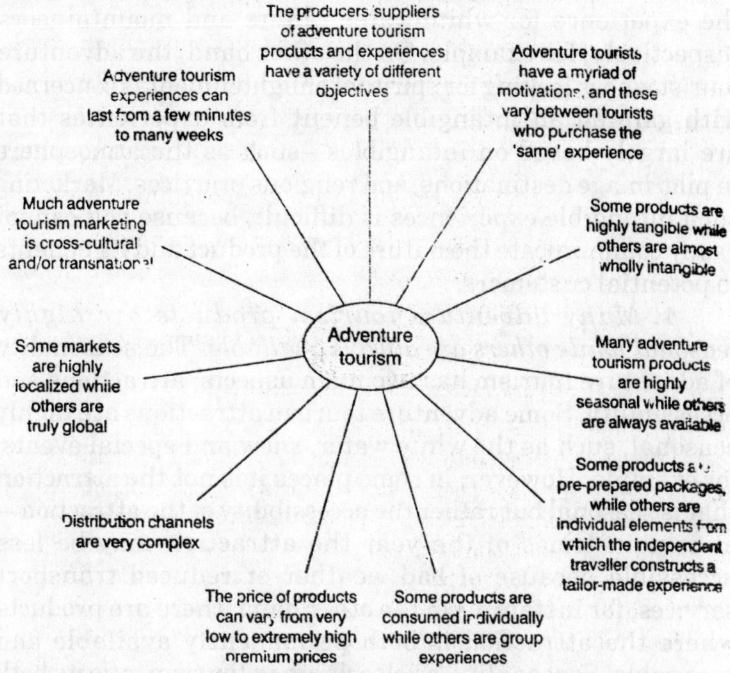

Fig. 8.1—The complexities of adventure tourism marketing.

2. *Adventure tourists have a myriad of motivations and these motivations vary between tourists purchasing the 'same' experience.* If you think about all the types of adventure tourism mentioned in this book and then try to 'brainstorm' motivations people could have for taking part in them, you will need a very large piece of paper or white board. Motivations could include everything from gaining status to the desire for sensual pleasure, escaping from the conventions of everyday life to meeting people, testing oneself to improving one's health. If we looked at any single group of people on a specific adventure tourism trip, then it is likely there would be significant differences between the motivations of each participant.

3. *Some products are highly tangible while others are almost wholly intangible.* Physical adventure trips tend to

rely heavily on tangible features such as rivers and mountains. These physical natural resources are the core of the experience for white-water rafters and mountaineers respectively, for example. On the other hand, the adventure tourist who is looking for spiritual enlightenment is concerned with gaining an intangible benefit from experiences that are largely based on intangibles—such as the atmosphere in pilgrimage destinations, and religious practices. Marketing such intangible experiences is difficult, because you cannot easily communicate the nature of the product and its benefits to potential customers.

4. *Many adventure tourism products are highly seasonal while others are always available.* The seasonality of adventure tourism has two main aspects; attractions and accessibility. Some adventure tourism attractions are highly seasonal, such as the white water, snow and special events, for example. However, in some places it is not the attraction that is seasonal but rather the accessibility of the attraction—at certain times of the year the attraction may be less accessible because of bad weather or reduced transport services, for instance. On the other hand, there are products where the attraction is both permanently available and accessible. Seasonality, as elsewhere in tourism, affects both pricing and the potential volume of demand.

5. *Some products are pre-prepared packages while others are individual elements from which the independent traveller constructs a tailor-made experience.* A single adventure tourism attraction can be part of a prepared package or can be selected by an independent traveller to be part of a personally tailor-made experience. This is true of everything from ski slopes to hunting reserves, visits to religious retreats to trips to desert regions. The same is of course also true of accommodation and transport services that are aimed at the adventure tourist.

6. *Some products are consumed individually while others are group experiences.* Many adventure tourism experiences are intensely personal, solo activities. Often, not only do these 'independent' tourists not want to take their vacation as part of a group but they would also prefer

it if there were no other tourists around at all in their destination environment. Conversely, a number of adventure experiences tend to be group activities with the enjoyment coming partly from the interaction between participants. This is clearly an important issue to bear in mind when promotional messages are being designed.

7. *The price of products can vary from very low to high premium pricing.* Some adventure tourism can be free, at least in terms of the use of natural attractions, for example. However, even in these areas most adventure tourism involves paying a price to use certain attractions, accommodation, transport and so on. Some products are aimed specifically at disadvantage sections of the community for social reasons, and these are low priced or may even be free to the consumer, thanks to public sector or voluntary sector subsidies. On the other hand, some adventure vacations are priced very highly as high status products. Interestingly, people on low-priced and high-priced trips may find themselves sharing the same core product, such as a mountain or a river, at the same time in the same weather.

8. *Distribution channels are often very complex.* The distribution of adventure tourism products often involves the use of numerous distribution channels. For example, imagine a small specialist adventure activity organiser in an established tourist destination. It could distribute its product as follows:

- Within the destination, directly, to individual customers who visit its office
- Within the destination, directly, to groups of customers who visit its office
- As 'tailor-made packages' for local hotels and travel agencies
- As 'tailor-made packages' for externally based tour operators
- Directly with individuals/groups via the Internet.

This range of different distribution channels has implications for the pricing of the product by the organiser, as well as for its promotional campaigns.

9. *Some markets are highly localised while others are truly global.* In some destinations, the majority of the adventure tourism market is local. This tends to be the case in countries or regions with a sizeable population and a developed economy, and which are a considerable distance from major tourism markets. Until recently this was the case with New Zealand, for instance. However, destinations are attracting an increasing number of people from other countries and even continents. There is now also a segment of tourists who are keen to take adventure holidays all over the world. Many destinations now have markets that are truly global. The geographical catchment area of a destination market clearly has great implications for its pricing, promotion and destination.

10. *Much adventure tourism marketing is cross-cultural and/or transnational.* The phenomenon of adventure tourism that crosses cultural and/or national boundaries is increasing due to the falling real cost of long-haul travel and the growing interest in adventure tourism in emerging outbound tourism markets. Where such cross-cultural tourism occurs it poses challenges for marketers, with a need to reconcile cultural differences between the destination and markets in terms of everything from concepts of what constitutes adventure to ethical standards, attitudes towards risk to dietary needs, food preferences, languages, and legal contracts concerning how products can be advertised.

11. *Adventure tourism experiences can last from a few minutes to many weeks.* Adventure experiences can last for a very short period, such as a few minutes in the case of bungee jumping or a flight in a Russian MiG fighter. This puts great pressure on the product to deliver instant satisfaction to the tourist. Conversely, trekking or overland expeditions can last for several weeks. Here the emphasis is on providing highlights throughout the trip to sustain satisfaction, as well as ensuring that the total cost is affordable for the target market.

Furthermore, we can identify a number of characteristics that distinguish marketing in adventure tourism from that in other sectors. These include the following:

- An emphasis on psychographic segmentation because so many of the motivators and determinants of the behaviour of adventure tourists relates to their personalities and lifestyles. It is clear that this fact is well understood by the adventure tourism industry just by looking at the brochures produced by specialist tourist operators in the field.
- Recognising the importance of bestowing status on purchasers of adventure tourism products is vital in the marketing in this sector. However, the concept of status clearly varies between different kinds of products and experiences. It may mean exclusively on the basis of the rarity value and uniqueness of the experience and/or high price. Alternatively, an adventure tourist may gain status from being away from other tourists or visiting exotic destinations at low cost as a budget traveller. Here, the lower the price paid the greater the status enjoyed by the tourist. This is particularly the case in the student backpacking market.
- Most adventure tourism marketing is carried out by small and medium-sized enterprises, whether tour operators, travel agencies or even destination marketing agencies. This is in contrast with many other sectors of tourism, where marketing is now dominated by large-scale, often trans-national companies.
- Specialist media play a significant role in promoting adventure tourism products and destinations. These specialist media include general adventure tourism magazines (such as *Wanderlust* in the UK) as well as periodicals that focus on one activity like

mountaineering or sailing. The modern types of destination guides, such as Lonely Planet and Rough Guides, also often promote adventure tourism opportunities within destinations.

- The Internet probably plays a greater role in adventure tourism marketing than it does in other sectors for several reasons. First, it is a form of promotion and distribution that suits small and medium enterprises that do not have the budget to produce glossy brochure and do not sell enough holidays to be attractive to travel agents. Second, in a rapidly changing business it allows producers regularly to update their selling messages, reflecting daily changes in snow conditions for example. Third, in a market that is truly global the Internet means that products and destinations can take bookings from clients anywhere in the world, day and night. Finally, the Internet is a relatively inexpensive form of promotion and it is very effective in targeting niche markets, like adventure tourism, effectively.
- With most adventure tourism products there is a great emphasis on brand loyalty and repeat business, as this is much less expensive than having constantly to find new customers in a numerically small specialist market.

We will now look at some other issues relating to the marketing of adventure tourism, beginning with market segmentation.

Segmentation and marketing

Segmentation is at the heart of modern marketing. No longer do we see markets as monolithic, homogeneous mass markets. Instead we divide the potential market into segments, or groups, who share similar characteristics. These characteristics can be geographical (*i.e.* where the tourists come from), demographic (age, sex, race and so on) and psychographic (lifestyle and personality).

The first two methods have traditionally been used in tourism, and for adventure tourism marketers there are interesting trends in relation to both:

- More and more people from countries that previously generated few adventure tourism trips, including Taiwan, South Korea, China, India and Russia, are now taking adventure vacations
- The growing number of empty nesters and senior citizens who are enjoying the benefits of improved health care, and are keen to try new adventure experiences, and are healthy enough to take part in them
- The increasing participation of women in adventurous travel, particularly some sports and backpacking
- The trend towards couple with children taking part in family adventure vacations.

At the same time psychographic segmentation is at the core of adventure tourism marketing, because personality type is a key determinant to whether or not people will take adventure trips. Adventurous risk-takers are more likely to take such vacations than cautious people. However, when designing products and promotional messages and industry needs to recognise that cautious, non-risk-takers may find themselves taking such trips to please their more adventurous partners and friends. These people may refuse to go on some trips unless they can be reassured that the vacation is safe.

Personality also plays a part in determining if people will travel individual or in groups, and whether they will take independent trips or buy organised packages.

The lifestyle of tourists also affects the type of adventure trip they will take. Often they will take a vacation that allows them to pursue an interest or hobby they enjoy at home, such as rock-climbing or partying. Alternatively, the adventure trip can be a total contrast with the everyday life of the tourist.

Adventure tourism organisations also have to recognise that there are 'shades' of adventure tourist, from the occasional participant in a particular type of activity to those who seek adventure in every moment of every holiday they take.

As we are about to talk about the Internet, it is worth saying that many believe that the opportunities for customised, targeted communication that the Internet offers mean that in future we will be able to treat every individual as a separate unique market segment.

The role of the Internet

The Internet is revolutionising the marketing of adventure tourism in several ways:

1 It allows small-scale tour operators to promote their produces at a minimal cost. This is important, given that such tour operators have not traditionally been able to sell via travel agents because of their low sales volume. Previously they have had to rely heavily on relatively expensive press advertisements and glossy brochures.
2 It provides an opportunity for entrepreneurs to regularly update their promotional message and prices in response to changes in market conditions.
3 It has changed the traditional 4 'Ps', or marketing mix, by combining promotion and place or distribution. Websites both provide information and allow the customer to make a reservation in a single transaction at the same time. This facilitates the spontaneous 'impulse purchase' decision.
4 Given that small operators are unable to staff reservation offices 24 hours a day, seven days a week, the Internet provides them with a low-cost way of taking bookings at all hours of the day and night. This is particularly important when selling on a global scale, where clients may live in countries in different time zones.

5 It is an effective tool for both relationship marketing and the targeting of small niche markets.
6 Guide book publishers, such as Lonely Planet, have set up their own websites that, while independent, recommend particular adventure tourism destinations and suppliers.
7 Many travellers are now creating their own websites or contributing to those set up by others, and on these sites their experiences are shared. This can help, indirectly, to promote particular adventure tourism destinations and operations; however, it can also have the opposite affect if the experiences were negative.

There seems little doubt that the Internet will play an increasing role in the marketing of adventure tourism because as Millington (2001) notes:

For the adventure travel operator, the Internet is proving to be the perfect mechanism for selling holidays. The profile of the average Internet user clearly matches that of a consumer who is likely to participate in adventure travel.

However, to be effective sites must be well designed and simple and quick to use, which is not always the case currently.

Promotional strategies

The promotional strategies used in the adventure tourism industry reflects the fact that most players within the sector are small and medium-sized enterprises. In other words, the emphasis is on finely targeted activities that maximize cost-effectiveness.

For the typical adventure travel tour operator, the promotional mix could include:

- The production of a relatively small number of glossy, high-quality brochures, which are not distributed widely but are instead only sent out in response to a specific enquiry. We will look at the brochures in a little more detail later.

- Websites featuring colourful images, factual information, and prices, together with a booking facility. There may also be a section containing testimonials from previous customers.
- Exhibiting at specialist adventure travel trade shows. Several UK cities now have at least one such show each year, where potential customers visit to look at what is on offer for the following year. One special exhibition in the UK, The Adventure Travel and Sports Show, attracted 2000 exhibitors and 28000 visitors in 2000 (Millington,2001).
- Direct mail marketing, particularly to past customers, to encourage brand loyalty and repeat purchase. Incentives may also be offered to existing customers who recommend new potential clients to the organisation.
- Trying to obtain favourable mentions of the company's products in the travel media, including newspapers, magazines and television programmes.
- Placing small advertisements in specialist magazines in the travel supplements of newspapers.
- Doing talks or film shows for potential clients.

However, the brochure still remains the mainstay of most adventure travel marketing, although this may change with the growth of the Internet.

Looking at these brochures, certain similar themes seem to emerge regardless of which company it is or which destination. Some of the main messages that are used in adventure travel brochures are illustrated in Table, through real extracts taken from five current brochures.

In adventure travel brochures, in general the companies are keen to reassure potential clients that they:

- Are experienced and have trained, highly skilled tour leaders
- Offer value for money
- Give the traveller extraordinary experiences

Table 8.1—Key messages in five selected adventure travel brochures

Message	*Brochure*
Experience more on small group exploratory holidays.	Explore World-wide 2002-2003
The Ultimate Adventure	Kumuka Expeditions 2001-2002
Discovery and Adventure	Exodus 2001-2002
Join us on one of the best holidays you will ever have—your world will never be the same again	Explore World-Wide 2002-2003
Small group adventures—how much fun can you handle?	AmeriCon Adventures 2001-2002
Our holidays are great fun, good value, professionally run, educational and responsible	Discover the World 2001-2002
By joining a Kumuka tour you can enjoy freedom as an individual traveller whilst having the back-up and support of our experience	Kumuka Expeditions 2001-2002
Get away from it all with American Adventures and Roadrunner!!	AmeriCon Adventures 2000-2002
Since 1974 we have been running trips for people who want to experience the world as well as see it	Exodus 2001-2002
There are prices to suit all pockets, from £420 to more than £6000	Discover the World 2001-2002
Warning! Adventure Travel can be habit-forming	Explore World-wide 2002-2003
Adventures for the young and young at heart	AmeriCon Adventures 2000-2002
We travel in small groups causing as little environmental impact and cultural disturbance as possible. We use local resources and services wherever possible making our tour itineraries individual enough to be a positive and sustainable alternative to mass tourism	Explore World-Wide 2002-2003
Experience Central and South America by travelling with local people and enjoying insights into the Latin lifestyle	Kumuka Expeditions 2001-2002
At Kumuka we know that your crew are the most important part of the tour. That is why we select our crew for their organisational skills, energy, and friendly personality. They undergo an extensive training programme, and as fellow travellers themselves, have a genuine, enthusiasm for travel	Kumuka Expeditions 2001-2002

Our groups are small and, unlike many other operators, wherever possible we charter boats exclusively to provide maximum space for observation and photography	Discover the World 2001-2002
We try at all times to ensure that all our trips are socially, economically, and ecologically sound, because these are the three essential issues of any responsible tour policy	Exodus 2001-2002
Our business thrives on word of mouth. The majority of our clients have either travelled with us before or have been recommended by friends and relatives	Discover the World 2001-2002
Our Leaders will not only look after the practitioners, they will also ensure that you enjoy your trip whatever happens	Exodus 2001-2002
Our tours have been thoroughly planned for our clients to enjoy value for money and to ensure that you take home life-long memories	Kumuka Expeditions 2001-2002
We are pleased to announce that in the inaugural Wanderlust Readers Travel Awards, Exodus was voted top tour operator	Exodus 2001-2002

- Do not arrange travel in large groups
- Are responsible organisations that are sensitive to the needs of the environment and host communities.

The brochures tend to differ from those of mass market tour operators in a number of ways:

- They focus less attention on prices and discounts and more on value for money and exclusivitly
- They provide much more detail on the itineraries and destinations
- They offer guidance on which kind of people each tour will suit rather than suggesting that they will appeal to everyone.

The marketing of adventure tourism destinations

Having focused on how individual companies market their adventure travel products, it is now time to consider the marketing of adventure tourism destinations.

The first thing to say is that there is much more adventure tourism going on than there was a few years ago. New destinations are being launched all the time as countries and regions seek to attract the economic benefits that such tourism can bring. However, like all destination marketing, the 'selling' of adventure tourism destinations is a complex matter for the following reasons:

1. Most marketing is undertaken by public sector destination marketing agencies who do not own or control much of the product and its pricing or distribution. Agencies therefore have to focus on the one element of the marketing mix they can control, or at least influence—namely promotion.
2. Some forms of adventure tourism are lucrative and controversial at the same time, notably wilderness hunting. Destination marketing agencies that publicly promote such products may alienate other types of tourists and make them go elsewhere.
3. Tourists perceptions of the identify of a particular destination may conflict with the boundaries adopted by the public sector bodies charged with marketing these destinations. For example, tourists may think of the Austrian Tyrol as a single entity, but it may be marketed by different individual municipalities with different (and perhaps conflicting) objectives and marketing strategies.
4. The perceptions about the destination held by potential visitors are largely influenced by external sources over which the destination has little or no control, such as foreign tour operators and the media.
5. Destination marketing in most countries is organised in a hierarchical fashion. National governments promote whole countries usually through a few key images of what are perceived to be the leading attractions of the country. Regional authorities often promote regions within countries, again highlighting their own selection of the leading

attractions. The individual municipalities or local government authorities seek to market their own corner of the region. There is often tension between the different geographical levels of marketing, and mixed, confusing messages are often given to the markets as a result.

6. Often the nature of adventure tourism in a particular destination changes from one season to the next. In a mountain area, winter means sküng, spring may be the peak season for white-water rafting, summer the time for hanggliding, and autumn the prime season for trekking. This means marketers have to modify the marketing mix several times during a single year to meet the needs of different market segments.

7 Adventure tourism is a very competitive business today, and therefore most adventure tourism destinations face considerable competition from:
   - Neighbouring regions in the same country with similar attractions
   - Regions elsewhere in the world that offer similar attractions
   - Regions elsewhere in the world that offer different attractions but similar benefits for tourists
   - Adventure sports and activities that 'tourists' can undertake in their home area.

It is not surprising, therefore, that destinations make great use of a range of promotional techniques such as advertising, brochures, press and public relations, and attendance trade fairs to try to sell the unique aspects of their destination.

9

Risk Management

Introduction

With a series of widely publicized incidents in recent years, risk management has become a major issue for organizations involved in all areas of adventure tourism–including adventure sports centres, specialist tour operators and trekking companies. At the same time, these organizations cannot eliminate the risk and also need to recognize that the risk itself is part of the motivation for most adventure tourists.

However, for adventure tourism organizations the failure to manage risk effectively can have four related, negative consequences, as we can see from Figure 9.1

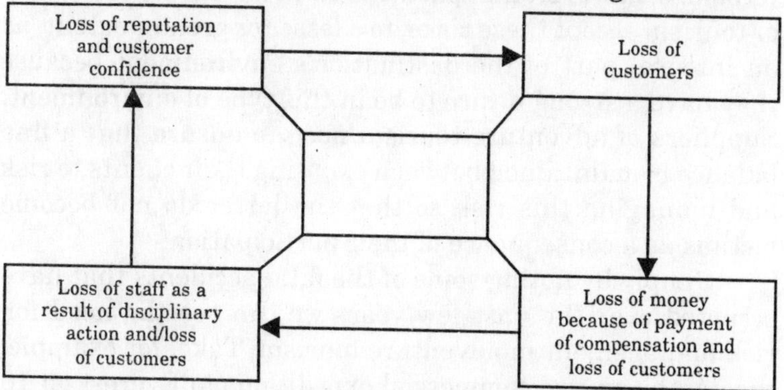

Fig. 9.1—The negative consequences of inadequate risk management.

In this chapter we will consider three aspects of the issue of risk management:

1. Risk management in a particular sector of physical adventure tourism, namely, mountain tourism. This section focuses on the duties of operators involved in this sector and concludes with general comments on the nature of risk that are also relevant to the rest of the chapter.
2. Risk management and independent physical adventure tourism.
3. The concept of risk management in non-physical adventure tourism.

The Final section of the chapter covers the issue of crisis management.

Risk management and mountain adventure Tourism

It is generally recognized that risk is a key feature of most adventure tourism activities. Some people, who would undoubtedly be classified into the hard adventure category, thrive from this element of risk and its associated 'nighs' caused by adrenaline rushing through their bodies and minds. Others enjoy a certain level of risk in their adventures, although some degree of perceived control is essential to their overall enjoyment of the experience. It is important to recognize, however, that participants in adventure recreation or tourism accept these risks, to a lesser or greater extent, as an integral part of the destination's environment because they have a strong desire to be in this type of environment. Suppliers of adventure tourism need to ensure that a fine balance is maintained between exposing their clients to risk and managing this risk so that the latter do not become victims as a consequence of their participation.

Simply by noting some of the fatal accidents that have occurred over the past few years we can see the need for risk management in adventure tourism: Take, for example, the deaths on two commercial expeditions to Everest on 10 May 1996 (Krakauer, 1997); the death of a porter in Nepal

1996 (Duff, 1998); the 21 deaths in the Swiss canyoning accident on 27 July 1999 (Dodd, 1999); and the death of a teenage girl on Mount Kinabalu in 2001. Indeed the necessity for risk management throughout the entire tourism industry is important, as 'the increased volume of global tourism activity has combined with the attractiveness of high risk exotic destinations to expose tourists to greater levels of risk' (Faulkner, 2001).

On the general theme of why accidents happen, some academics adopt a human psychology approach to causation–such as Reason's (1990) study of human error and his development of the generic modelling system. In contrast, others take an organizational approach, For instance, Turner (1979, 1994) accepts that accidents are often sparked by a technical failure, but believes that they are amplified by the institutional, administrative and organizational context within which they occur. Whilst theorists have sought to understand why accidents happen, the real task of risk management is to develop strategies to prevent or minimize these for individual organizations.

Although a body of literature exists on the generic theme of risk management, research into the use of this management technique within the tourism industry and more specifically within the adventure travel sector is sparser. However, there are several useful studies that have contributed knowledge to risk management in tourism. For instance, Hollman and Forrest (1991) developed a model to explain risk management in service companies (tourism is a service industry *par excellence*) on the basis that 'risk management involves the protection of a firm's assets and profits'. The model is a five-stage process involving the discovery of loss exposure, the evaluation of loss exposure, operational techniques, implementation of strategy and monitoring. Risk-management strategies are divided into two broad categories: 'operational techniques' are measures that reduce loss exposure, for example fire-fighting equipment; and 'financing techniques' aim to minimize the effects of loss on a business, for instance transferring the financial consequences of loss to an insurer.

Though Faulkner (2001) acknowledges the vulnerability of tourism to natural disasters and terrorism, he argues that 'few tourism organizations at the enterprise of destination level have properly developed disaster strategies as an integral part of their business plan'. He proposes a 'tourism disaster management framework that involves formulating disaster contingency plans based on risk assessment of both potential disasters and the probability of their occurrence'.

In an attempt to determine appropriate risk management strategies for tourist scuba-diving operations, Wilks and Davis (2000) developed a risk evaluation matrix. The matrix entails four components: risk retention is the assumption or acceptance of loss by the operator; risk transfer is the use of insurance to cover infrequent but potentially costly accidents; risk reduction is the adoption of 'best practice' to keep the likelihood of accidents to a minimum; and risk avoidance is achieved by eliminating those activities that are too risky from the operators' product portfolio.

Frequency of risk potential		
High	Reduce risk	Avoid risk
Low	Retain risk	Transfer risk

Fig. 9.2—Risk evaluation matrix (Willks and Davis, 2000: 595).

The conclusion that Morgan (2000) draws from an investigation into whitewater rafting in New Zealand is that operators target an optimal safety level through an assessment of the desired level of risk. The assessment involves numerous criteria, including the technical abilities of employees, the standard and type of equipment used, the physical location of the activity and legal obligations. Operators have to 'estimate the level of actual control that participants will require to meet the actual risks from the physical hazards to be encountered'. Furthermore, operators have some influence over the client's perception of risk; guides can talk the risks up to make the experience seem more exciting or talk them down to avoid over-arousal and subsequent loss of control by the clients. Clients can enjoy an optimal adventure experience so long as the operator understands clients' expectations and their perceived levels of risk in the activity.

Priest and Gass (1997) examined risk management in outdoor education a sector that is closely linked to adventure tourism. They view risk management as the:

> ...policies., practices and procedures used...to appropriately address potential personal injury and financial losses, protecting [the] adventure organization from the economic cost of being such and reducing [the] organization's financial obligation if a suit is successful.

They argue that accidents are a result of the interaction between environmental dangers, objective hazards that arise from the local environment and human dangers—subjective perils within human control. To illustrate this, consider an alpine ascent where objective dangers exist in the form of crevasses. High temperature cause these ice formations to be less stable, resulting in a greater accident potential. This can be reduced by crossing the danger zone at night when temperature are lowest. The authors propose a ten-step plan for assessing dangers in outdoor education environments (see table 9.1), although these procedures are not always adhered to due to a number of inhibiting factors. These include: the unfamiliarity of new or unexpected situations, 'smelling the barn' (*i.e.* the rush to get home when the activity is nearly complete) and a relaxation of concentration caused by fatigue, carelessness or over-familiarity.

Table 9.1— Procedure for analysis dangers (Priest and Gass, 1997)

Step	Explanation
1. Plan ahead	Recognize that accidents with happen; pre-plan
2. Identify dangers	Be continuously aware of dangerous situations and conditions
3. Point out potential dangers	Ensure that all group members are aware of the existence of potential dangers once identified
4. When appropriate, remove elements that contribute to dangerous situations	If warning does not adequately deal with the danger, remove it as long as it does not increase risk
5. Avoid dangerous situations	Change pre-planned activity or route to safer alternative if possible
6. Identify and classify dangerous situations	What are the perils and hazards? How can hazards be minimized?
7. Assess risk and reclassify danger	Are the dangers environmental or human?
8. Estimate potential losses	What are the number and strength of dangers?
9. Minimize losses	Adopt course of action that keeps the accident outcome as acceptable and recoverable as possible
10. Make appropriate adjustments	Adopt pre-planned accident countermeasures.

The four risk management strategies identified in the risk evaluation matrix by Wilks and Davis (2000); Figure 9.2) are similarly employed by Priest and Gass. They view litigation as a key consideration for outdoor education providers, in which liability is defined as 'the degree of legal responsibility or obligation that people or programmes have for repairing damages (often by paying money) for injuries to participants' (Priest and Gass, 1997: 124). In the context of mountain adventure tourism, the tort of negligence is the most applicable—*i.e.* 'unintentional breach of legal duty causing damage reasonably foreseeable without which breach the damage would not have occurred' (Van der Smissen, 1990: quoted in Priest and Gass, 1997). However, providers can avoid lawsuits through adopting various measures. One measure is to aim to prevent the accident in the first place by having proper safety procedures. This would act as a good defence should a case arise, illustrating to courts that the operation was conducted professionally. Another defence is to inform clients fully of the potential risks and likelihood of accidents involved in the adventure activity. Priest and Gass conclude that a postaccident strategy is paramount to effective risk management. This should include such measures as first aid, evacuation procedures and keeping accurate records of incidents.

Brown (1999) also approaches risk management from an outdoor education perspective. His Adventure REACT model involves 'the recognition, evaluation, adjustment, choice and tracking phases of risk management' and the associated risk-management strategies are again based on retention, reduction, avoidance and transferal of risk. Brown stresses the need for an effective critical incident management plan' that should address staff responsibilities and task, communication protocols, first aid and rescue procedures, evacuation policies and procedures for fatality management. However, he accepts that 'safety cannot necessarily be guaranteed by a set of rigid standards' due to the fact that objective dangers exist that are difficult to control. In essence, no matter how good the risk management plan is, it is impossible to avoid every single risk.

In the same vein, Cloutier (2000) affirms that risk is an innate component of all adventure activities and hence risk management 'is about managing or optimizing risk' rather than abolishing it completely.

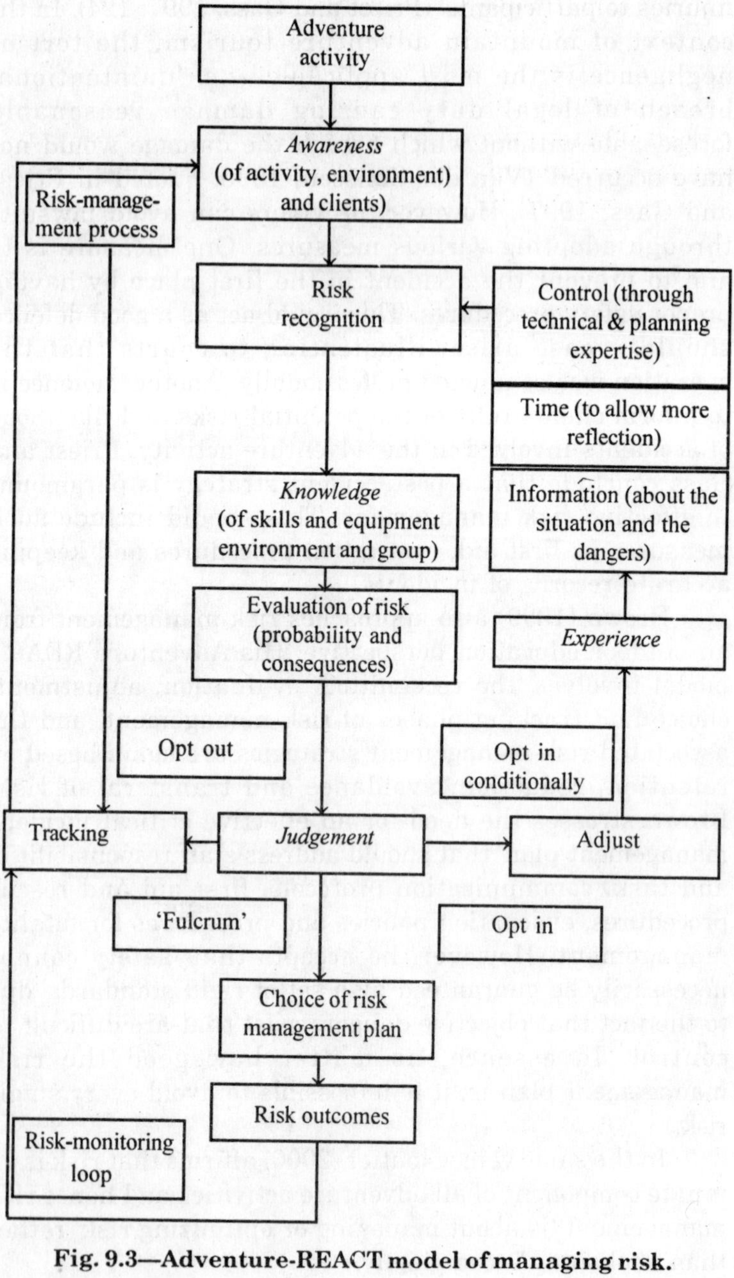

Fig. 9.3—Adventure-REACT model of managing risk.

Therefore, for the activity to remain adventurous the risk management process needs to determine acceptable exposure levels for clients and operators alike, identify risks, select suitable risk-management strategies, implement these and make the appropriate responses to incidents. Cloutier (1998, 2000) divides risk management strategies into two broad approaches. Risk control concerns the decision not to undertake a trip or activity due to the high risk involved. It also refers to risk-reduction measures such as client briefings and increasing instructional ratios for activities considered of greater risk. Risk financing follows on from risk control and involves both risk retention and risk transfer. He recommends the preparation of an 'emergency response plan' (Cloutier, 1998: 1-2) for each trip, comprising risk management objectives, identification of hazards, evaluation of hazards, risk-management strategies, incident response strategies, action plan and controls. A number of techniques can be used to ascertain hazards–for examples, site inspections and hazard checklists. In evaluating hazards, providers should examine the frequency and severity of their occurrence and consequently 'assign a high, medium, low priority to each and create strategies to mitigate their effects' (Cloutier, 1998: 7). The incident response strategy should clearly set out the roles and responsibilities within the organization in the case of an incident, considering such factors as identifying the staff member who would mobilize and activate the incident response strategy.

A model of risk Management

Whilst the aforementioned studies provide clear guidelines on what adventure operators should do in terms of their risk management strategies, only a limited amount of actual primary research has been conducted in this field. Cloutier's (1998) work, for instance, is written from the perspective of advising his students as to which methods they should adopt. In a bid to ascertain how the risk management process operates in practice, Hibbert

(2001) conducted an investigation into the mountain adventure tourism sector. He undertook a series of in-depth interviews with tour operators who offered mountain adventure products and in addition sought the views of the governing body of British mountaineering, the British Mountaineering Council (BMC). A model of 'risk management practice in mountain adventure tourism' emerged from these primary findings. The model incorporates contemporary viewpoints drawn from risk management literature and details specific risk management strategies that mountain adventure tourism operators employ in practice. A broad overview of the interview results and recommendations is presented here.

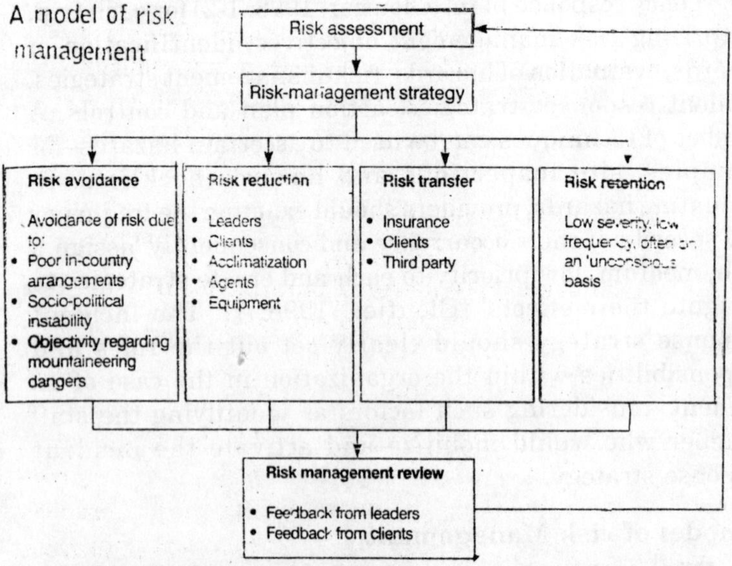

Fig. 9.4—Model of risk management practice in mountain adventure tourism (after British Mountaineering Council).

Risk Assessment

All operators considered the elements of risk involved in their adventure products at the trip planning stage. At the same time, it was recognized that unforeseen risks could occur on a day-to-day basis throughout the trips. Hibbert

(2001) concluded that most mountain adventure risk management is conducted during the actual trips rather than in the company's office beforehand. Some operators assessed risk through reconnaissance trips to the destination. As one operator explained, 'it's the first-hand experience that proves how much of a risk the trip is likely to be'. Hibbert advocates the implementation of formal written risk mangement planning, based on Cloutier's (2000) argument that it 'forces the business manager to think through individual and corporate philosophies, acceptable procedures and legal-liability ramifications'.

The model incorporates the four risk management strategies identified in previous research:

1. *Risk avoidance.* Operators employ this strategy when there are poor in-country arrangements, socio-political instability at the destination, or objective mountaineering dangers. The latter hazards are specific to mountain environments and are usually byond a person's control. An example of this can be seen in one of the operator's trips to Naya Kanga, where the higher than normal temperatures and lack of snow cover led to an increased objective danger of stone fall to a level that was deemed unacceptable. Risk avoidance can also be achieved through offering a trip in an alternative format. For example, one operator offers a trip to the Karakorum region of Pakistan, visiting the site of the K2 base camp and crossing the high pass of the Gondor La, while most companies offer this trek by ascending the Baltoro Glacier and then crossing the pass and dropping into the Huche Valley. The first operator goes the other way round due to the risk of stone fall in the pass. Ascending from the Huche Valley increases the chances of getting over the pass early in the morning whilst the rocks on the surrounding slopes are still frozen in place, thus reducing the objective danger.

2. *Risk reduction.* Operations utilize a number of risk reduction strategies. They look for trek leaders who have appropriate qualifications, as qualifications serve as an indication that leaders have a minimum level of experience

and have undertaken some formal training in practical mountaineering skills and party management. Leaders also need to be mentally robust enough to make unpopular decisions to ensoure the safety of their clients. In Hibbert's research, operators stressed the importance of clients choosing the right trip in accordance with their experience, skills etc. This was achieved through requesting clients to provide an outline of their experience before booking the trip. Some operators also assessed their clients' capabilities during the early part of a trip before committing to the main objective. In addition, operators assigned grades to their trips, to assist clients in making the correct choice. However, Hibbert notes that no uniform system of grading is available and hence clients may face problems when comparing the holiday products of one company against another. As many mountain adventure tourism activities involve clients being at high altitude, an acclimatization programme is necessary to reduce the risk of altitude sickness. Operators stressed that trips should be of an adequate length to ensure clients' acclimatization. Local agents were seen as key to risk reduction and whilst some operators had established good working relationships with these companies over several years they also noted difficulties in finding agents in whom they had compete confidence when breaking into new destinations.

3. *Risk transfer*. The transfer of risk from the operator to others is a key method used in managing risk (Hollman and Forest, 1991; Rest and Gass, 1997: Wilks and Davis, 2000). In Hibbert's study, operators identified three ways in which risks were transferred out: to the operators' own insurers, to the clients and to third parties. Transferring risk to insurance companies is the main method used and operators must hold public liability insurance as a legal requirement. All operators encouraged clients to recognize the risks involved in any particular trip. For instance, in the booking conditions one operator states: 'Place understand that there are certain hazards involved in climbing expeditions, which you must accept at your own risk. The

company will not be liable for any illness, injury or death sustained during an expedition, nor will it be liable for any uninsured losses of your property'. On the issue of transferring risk to third parties, operators used different measures. For instance, one company did not transfer any risks to third parties whilst another transferred some risk to its local agents indirectly through imposing financial penalties if a trip had serious problems.

4. *Risk retention.* Risk retention occurs where risk is not transferred to others and is accepted deliberately, either unconsciously or owing to the inability to transfer it to others (Clouter, 1998). It usually covers those risks that are low in both severity and frequency (Wilks and Davis, 2000). Risk retention did not seem to form a major part of the risk management strategies of operators. Hibbert notes that operators may take risks on unconsciously, for example one operator commented that some risk in loss of equipment was 'part and parcel' of the operation. This would explain the lack of risk retention strategies.

Hibbert also investigated how operators deal with the issues of litigation and emergency planning. The importance of having a strategy to avoid litigation was recognized by operators. As one operator commented, 'you can't get into this game without accepting at some point someone may possibly sue you or there may be a problem that may require a call on your professional indemnity insurance'. Three methods of dealing with litigation emerged: the avoidance of accidents through risk management strategies, a willingness to settle small claims out of court if it was felt the client had a case and financial protection from the consequences of litigation through insurance. Emergency plans differed according to the destinations, but were greatly affected by local conditions. The contrast between Nepal (where helicopter rescue was fairly advanced) and Bolivia and Mongolia (where such facilities were minimal or non-existent) was made by operators. This meant that local agents who could advise on the necessary arrangements were particularly important.

Risk Management Review

The risk management review forms the final component of the mode. Within any management system, a feedback loop that allows operations to be reviewed and procedures and policies to be modified in the light of experience is vital. Some operators stated that it was a formal requirement for their leaders to submit a written report at the end of each trip as part of their contracts, whilst others used a verbal reporting format. Client questionnaires were also completed post-trip by a number of operators and, whilst no specific safety comments were requested, all operators felt that any concerns would be brought up.

Risk management and independent physical adventure tourism

The previous section focuses on mountain tourism that is largely group-based and involves commercial and not-for-profit operators offering services to mountain adventure tourists. However, a major component of physical adventure tourism is independent travel rather than being organized by specialist operators. Individuals or groups make their own arrangements and are therefore also responsible for their own risk management.

If we imagine a group of friends who want to take a trip heli-skiing in the Caucasus Mountains, the potential risks they face are many and varied, including:

- Financial risks, if, for example, they book their travel before they obtain a visa, then discover they will not get visas and cannot claim a reimbursement of their travel costs.
- Health risks in terms of disease (such as diphtheria), illness (such as food poisoning) or injury.
- Safety risks, such as travelling in inadequately maintained helicopters in difficult terrain, or kidnapping by terrorist groups.

They will endeavour to manage this risk as best they can by:

- Reducing the risks where possible—for instance, they may consult guidebooks, government embassies and websites to gain information that will help them be better prepared for their trip.
- Putting plans in place to ensure that if the worst does happen, the damage is minimal—this may, for example, involve purchasing specialist medical insurance that guarantees evacuation by all in the event of an accident on the slopes.

As in any risk management situation, our group of intrepid skiers will need to balance the benefits of taking such actions with the financial and time costs involved. This means they will need to carry out an evaluation of the chance that a particular risk will become a reality against the severity of the consequences if it does happen.

To reduce the risk while maintaining predominantly independent quality of the tourism experience, they may hire a local guide for part of their time in the Caucasus. On the other hand, they may relish the idea of the riskiness of endeavouring to take a trip where they are wholly reliant on their own abilities.

Whatever approach they take, they will also need to develop their own formal (or more likely informal) guidelines covering the responsibilities of each group member towards fellow travellers is terms of the management of risk. Will they make a group decision, for instance, to avoid particularly dangerous slopes, or will each individual member make an individual choice? If the latter, will the individual concerned expect the others to attempt a rescue if anything goes wrong?

It is easy to try to answer such questions while sitting at home planning such a trip, but it is very different when tourists are on the slopes, with the adrenaline pulsing through their veins!

The concept of risk management in non-physical adventure tourism

Most analysis of risk in adventure tourism focuses on physical adventure tourism. However, not all adventure tourism is physical in nature, and nor are the risks of adventure tourism always physical. Table 9.2 endeavours to illustrate this point by looking at different types of nonphysical adventure tourism, the risks involved, and how tourists can seek to manage these risks.

The risks identified in Table 9.2 are, of course, in addition to the normal risks involved in all travel.

It must also be recognized that in any situations there will be those who perceive no risks and accordingly practise no approach to risk management at all. At the same time, we must note that the division between physical and non-physical adventure tourism and risks is largely artificial. In most cases adventure tourism has both physical and non-physical elements, and the risks associated with it are of both types too. For example, a young female backpacker travelling through. South-East Asia faces both physical risks (attack or illness) and non-physical risks (verbal sexual harassment and the constant attention of beggars.)

Having looked at the nature of risk, it is now time to move on to the assoicated subject of crisis management.

Crisis management

Crisis management is about what happens when the risk becomes reality. It is always better to develop crisis management plans in advance of the crisis, rather than managing it in an *ad hoc* manner in the 'heat of the moment'.

Organizations such as specialist tour operators need crisis management plans for all foreseeable emergencies. These should be written down and communicated to all staff so that when a crisis occurs everyone knows exactly what to do. The plan should, for example, say what will happen in the event of the drowning of a client on a white-water rafting trip, including:

Table 9.2 The risks involved in non-physical adventure tourism

Type of adventure tourism	*Nature of risk*	*Approaches to risk management*
1. Hedonistic tourism	• Sexually transmitted diseases • Alcohol poisoning • Getting involved in fighting • Arrest by the police for bad behaviour	• Don't care; will take no precautions and will deal with problems only if and when they arise • Go with friends for mutual support. • Take precautions such as using contraception in the event of indulging in casual sex.
2. Travelling another country to study	• Could fail due to lack of knowledge of other country's language and learning culture, with resulting loss of face. • Possible inability to integrate into host community/potential rejection by fellow students	• Careful choice of country and educational institution, which may mean choosing a country with the same language. • Prepare for the study abroad by improving language skills • Make a concentrated effort to fit into the host culture.
3. Gambling tourism	• Losing more money than one can afford • Becoming the victim of criminals.	• Only take a certain amount of money • Only go with friends who can offer support or control your behaviour • Avoid particularly risky casinos or neighbourhoods
4. Travelling in search of spiritual enlightenment	• The experience could, in extreme cases, lead to psychological problms and a sense of isolation from your own family, community and background • The chance of perhaps losing money to charlatans.	• You may not see any potential risk • Choose to travel with others for mutual support • Only visit places with established reputations.
5. Travelling to learn a new skill, such as cookery or craft-making	• You may dislike the activity and therefore gain little benefit from the expenditure of time and money	• Choose a skill you already have some interest in • Only choose a vacation package that is recommended by acquaintances, guidebooks or professional bodies.

- Who will inform the relatives and how?
- Whether the press will be informed and, if so, what will be said and who will say it.
- How the authorities will be informed of the event and by whom?

- Whether the trip should continue or be terminated immediately for all participants.
- What communication should take place with other clients on the same trip, and what counselling should be made available to them.
- All the relevant information (key telephone numbers, etc.) should be in an easily accessible crisis management file.
- Crisis management is a specialist field in its own right, but some general rules can perhaps be elucidated, such as:
- Staff who have been directly involved in the tragedy should *not* talk to the media, as they are too emotionally involved.
- Only one trained, experienced spokesperson should speak on behalf of the company.
- No speculation should be entered into about possible causes or the tragedy before a full enquiry has taken place.
- No suggestion of liability should be even hinted at before the completion of the aforementioned enquiry.

Even individual and independent adventure travellers need informal crisis management plans—idea of what they will do if thing go wrong. For many travellers, this may simply be calling their insurance company, friends or parents!

For many adventure tourists, dealing with a crisis or potential crisis enhances their enjoyment of a trip. On the other hand, failing to deal with it can ultimately ruin the trip or have even more tragic consequences.

10

The External Environment for Travel and Tourism Organizations—The Macro Context

Introduction

The most widely used technique for analysing the macro-environment is known as STEEP analysis. STEEP analysis divides the influences in the macro-environment into five categories:

Socio-demographic—social, cultural and demographic forces.

Technological influences—products, processes, IT, communications and transport.

Economic influences—fiscal and monetary policy, incomes, living standards, exchange rates etc.

Environmental influences—waste disposal, pollution and energy consumption.

Political influences—governmental, legal and regulatory influences.

It is worth noting that in some texts the STEEP acronym is replaced by STEP with environmental influences omitted. In other texts the STEP acronym is turned around and presented as PEST. However, the framework for analysis is essentially the same in both cases. It is this popular framework which is explained and explored in this chapter.

After studying this chapter, students should be able to:

- Explain what is meant by the macro-environment.
- Explain Ginter and Duncan's mechanisms of carrying out macro-environmental analysis.
- Describe the components of each of the four STEEP influences.
- Describe how the STEEP factors are interlinked and interrelated.

The Macroenvironment

What is the macroenvironment?

We refer to the macro-environment as the broad environment outside of an organization's industry and markets, It is generally beyond the influence of the individual organization but can have significant impact on the macro-environment (industry and market) in which the organization operates. The macro-environment is sometimes referred to as the *far* or *remote* environment because it tends to exert forces from outside the organization's sphere of influence and the forces are usually beyond control.

Changes in the macro-environment can be of immense importance to an organization. They can bring about the birth or death of an entire industry, they can make markets expand or contract, they can determine the level of competitiveness within an industry and many other things. It is therefore essential that managers are alert to actual and potential changes in the macro-environment and that they anticipate the potential impacts on their industry and markets. In many ways analysis of the macro-environment is more difficult than internal analysis since it involves everything that occurs outside the organization. The problems when dealing with such a vast amount of information are, first, assessing what should be included and what should be left out and second, how the information should be organized in a rational and meaningful way. As Lynch (2000: 109) made clear, 'there are no simple rules governing an analysis of the organization. Each analysis [of the macro-environment] needs to be guided by what is relevant for that particular organization. This is to say that although analytical frameworks can be suggested for sorting and organizing pertinent information, the key issues are likely to be highly specific to each organization's circumstances.

Conducting macro-environmental analysis

Ginter and Duncan (1990) listed the following activities as components of macro-environmental analysis:

- *Scanning* macro—environments for warning signs and possible environmental changes that will effect the business.
- *Monitoring*—environments for specific trends and patterns.
- *Forecasting*—future directions of environmental changes.
- *Assessing* current and future trends in terms of the effects such changes would have on the organization.

The same authors went on to identify the potential benefits of macro-environmental analysis as:

- Increasing managerial awareness of environmental changes.
- Increasing understanding of the context in which industries and markets function.
- Increasing understanding of multinational settings.
- Improving resource allocation decisions.
- Facilitating risk management.
- Focusing attention on the primary influences on strategic change.
- Acting as an early warning system, proving time to anticipate opportunities and threats and devise appropriate responses.

Limitations of macro-environmental analysis

We should be careful to note that macro-environmental analysis has its limitations and pitfalls. At its roots, the macro-environment can be extremely complex and at any one time there may be conflicting and contradictory changes taking place. The pace of change in many macro-environment situations is increasing and becoming more turbulent and unpredictable. This degree of uncertainty has, to some extent, cast some doubt over the value of carrying out a macro-environmental analysis at all. By the time that an organization has come to terms with one major change in the macro-environment, another change may have occurred that requires even more attention and action.

Accordingly, managers that are concerned with strategic analysis must:

- be aware of the limitations and inaccuracies of macro-environmental analysis;
- carry out the analysis continuously (because it changes so frequently);
- constantly seek to improve sources of information and techniques for its analysis;
- use the information as one source of organizational learning;
- use the information to inform future strategy.

With these points in mind, macro-environmental analysis is a valuable mechanism for increasing strategic awareness of managers.

STEEP Analysis

Overview of the STEEP Influences

The complexity of the macro-environment makes it necessary to divide the forces at work into the five broad categories we have already encountered. It is important to remember that the four categories are interrelated and constantly interact with each other. In the process of STEEP analysis (sometimes called STEP or PEST analysis) it is therefore important to explore and understand the relationships between the forces at work. It is equally important to identify the relative important of the influences at work for the organization, its industry and its markets. Finally, because of the uncertainty of the effects of macro-environmental change on the macro-environment, it is essential that a range of possible outcomes of the changes are identified and considered.

In carrying out a STEEP analysis it should be pointed out that some of the factors may be generic in that they affect all industrial sectors, whist other are specific to travel and tourism, or a particular sector within the industry. Peattie and Moutinho (2000) provided a review of some of the major environmental influences in travel and tourism using an extended framework, which they termed SCEPTICAL analysis. In this case the acronym stands for:

Social
Cultural
Economic
Physical
Technical
International
Communications and infrastructure
Administrative and institutional
Legal and political

Other texts such as Lockwood and Medlik (2001), Buhalis (2001), Vogel (2001), Cooper and Gilbert (1998) and Vanhove (2001) also give some interesting insights in discussing the key macro-environmental factors affecting the travel and tourism industry.

In her analysis, Auliana Poon (1993) pointed to the radical changes that were changing the travel and tourism industry. She suggested that a 'new tourism' was developing to replace the 'old tourism' based on mass tourism. The five key forces (consumers, technology, production, management and 'frame conditions') which had served to create mass tourism in the first place were themselves changing to create the new tourism. Figure 10.1 summarizes some of the changes taking place.

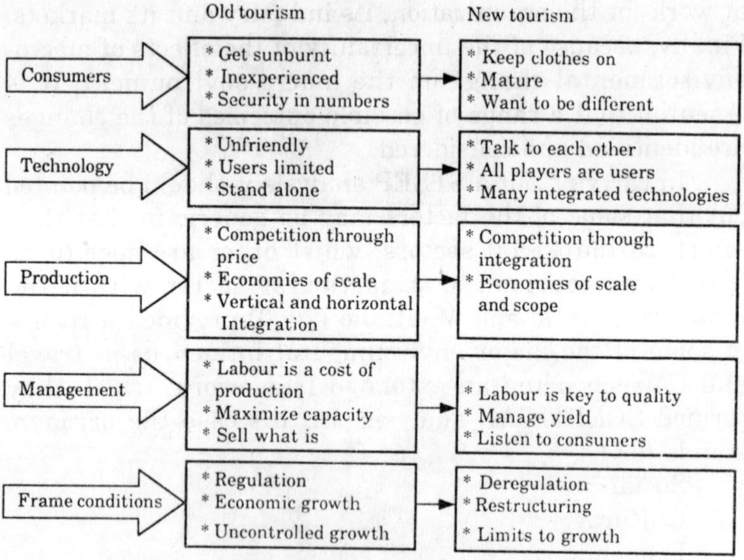

Fig. 10.1—Old and new tourism compared (adapted from Poon, 1993)

Some text use the STEP or PEST acronym, thereby omitting explicit recognition of physical environmental influences but considering these as part of the other influences. The approach here, however, is to explicitly recognize the central importance of physical environmental influences in a tourism context by considering them under a separate heading. It is clearly the case that there can be few industries where the interdependence between the physical environment and economic activity is so clearly visible (Peattie and Moutinho, 2000).

In the following sections the component parts of STEEP are considered systematically. The approach adopted here is to list some of the generic factors and to provide illustrations of the industry specific factors by using the airline industry for purposes of illustration.

Socio-demographic Influences

Analysis of the social environment is concerned with understanding the potential impacts of society and social changes on a business, its industry and markets.

For most analyses, analysis of the social environment will require consideration of :

* *Social culture* (values, attitudes and beliefs)–its impact on demand for products and services, attitudes to work, saving and investment, ecology, ethics, etc.
* *Demography*–the impact of the size and structure of the population on the workforce and patterns of demand.
* *Social structure*–its impact on attitudes to work and products and services.

Social culture

The cultures of countries in which a business operates can be of particular importance. The culture of a country consists of the values, attitudes and beliefs of its people, which will affect the way that they act and behave (or, put simply, its 'personality'). There are important cultural differences between all countries. Culture can affect consumer tastes and preferences, attitudes to work, attitudes to education and training, attitudes to corruption and ethics, attitudes to credit, attitudes to the social role of a business in society and many other things.

Demography

Demographic trends are similarly improtant. Demography is the social science concerned with the charting of the size and structure of a population of people. The size of the population will obviously be a determinant of the size of the workforce and the potential size of markets. Just as important will be the structure of the population. The age structure will determine the size of particular segments and also the size of the working population. The size and structure of the population will constantly be changing and these changes will have an impact on industries and markets.

Social Structure

Social structure is strongly linked to demography and refers to the ways in which the social groups in a population are organized. There are a number of ways of defining, social structure, such as by socio-demographic groupings, by age, sex, location, population density in different areas, etc. The social structure will affect people's lifestyles and expectations and so will strongly influence their attitudes to work and their demand for particular products and services.

Among the most important general changes in recent years in the social environment has been the change in people's attitudes to the physical environment. Increasing awareness of the problems caused by pollution and the exhaustion of non-renewable resources have caused travel and tourism organization to rethink (in many cases) the ways that they produce their products and the composition of the products themselves. Similarly, changes in social structure (upward mobility), lifestyle (increased leisure) and demography (ageing populations in developed countries) have significantly altered many market and industry structures.

Socio-demographic Influences—Airline Sector

A number of demographic factors point towards a greater use of air travel. Thus an increasing proportion of the population being relatively healthy and prosperous, increasing number of retired people, a decline in average family size, increasing amounts of paid holidays and larger numbers of double income families all point to higher usage of air services. Leisure travel (which accounts for about 80% of trips) has grown more rapidly than business based travel.

Other factors that might be considered are lifestlye trends and attitudes of society towards air travel and associated airport development. An increasingly mobile society where people take safe, reliable and affordable air transportation for granted is challenged by a critical society which assesses the contribution of air travel to air and noise pollution (Holloway, 1998). This dichotomy, in which the competing needs and interests of airline stakeholder groups need to be considered, represents a challenge to airlines, regulators and governments.

Technological Influences

Analysis of the technological environment involves developing an understanding of the effects of changes in technology on all areas of a business and its activities, including:

* Goods and services.
* Operational processes.
* Information and communications.
* Transport and distribution.
* Society, politics and economics.

Developments in information and communications technology (ICT), like the development of personal computers (PCs), networks, satellite, cable, Internet and digital communications together with rapid advances in software, have all contributed to revolutionizing the way that business in conducted in many industries. Activities are now better co-ordinated, research and development is speeded up, thus making businesses more flexible and responsive. For example, many activities previously carried out by middle layers of managers, which often involved collating and analysing data from operational activities and reporting to senior managers can now be more effectively carried out using ICT solutions. As a result, many companies such as British Airways have cut costs through reducing the numbers of people employed particularly at middle levels of the organization in a process referred to as *de-layering*.

Similarly, changes in transport technology have revolutionized business and have changed societies and cultures. It is possible to transport tourists as well as materials, components and products with far greater speed and at much lower cost as a result of developments in road, rail, sea and air transport. These improvement in transport have also increased the total amount of personal and business travel that people undertake and this has led to profound societal changes both in tourist 'exporting' and 'importing' regions. Increasing wine consumption and more varied culinary tastes in the UK are responses (at least in part), to wider participation in international travel.

As a consequence, it is important that organizations monitor changes in the technologies that can affect their operations or their markets. In most industries, organizations must be flexible and be ready to innovate and adopt new technologies as they come along. The way in which (and the extent to which) organizations do or do not employ the latest technology can be an important determinant of competitive advantage.

Technological influences—airline sector

The Computer Reservation Systems (CRS) such as Sabre developed by American Airlines are powerful tools of travel marketing technology. The system developed largely in the 1960s and 1970s have attained global reach and hence they are now often referred to as Global Distribution System (GDS). The recent development of Internet search and booking engines developed by CRS providers allow for diversified distribution and communication channels to be utilized thus creating new opportunities for airline marketing. Allied to the use of CRS are the Revenue Management Systems that have been developed. These systems, which utilize the CRS accumulated databases, allow for the yield realized to be optimized by varying prices and altering the mix between classes of tickets that are issued.

In relation to the aircraft themselves, technological innovations continue to drive costs down and influence route structures. The 380 (*Megaliner*) currently being developed by Airbus Industries, for example, will have a capacity of some 550 passengers with operating costs about 17% lower than the Boeing 747 (Brown, 2001). Route patterns and airport infrastructures are two aspects which may well have to change in response to the aircraft's introduction. Additionally, a number of short to medium range jet aircraft models with twin fuel efficient lean burn engines have been introduced over recent years and further such developments are planned. Such aircraft allow the airlines to consider introducing routes which were previously considered to be unviable.

Economic influences

Analysis of the economic environment will centre on changes in the macro-economy and their effects on business and consumers. It is important to remember that because governments intervene (to varying extents) in the operation of all countries' economies, many factors classed as political in this chapter will have important economic implications.

Broadly speaking, the regulation of a national economy is brought about by two key policy instruments—fiscal and monetary policy. These policy instruments, alongside influences from international markets, determine the economic climate in the country in which a business competes. From these, a number of other, vital economic indicators 'flow' and it is these that organizations experience–either for good or ill.

Concepts : Fiscal and Monetary Policy

Fiscal policy is the regulation of the national economy through the management of government revenues and expenditures. Each fiscal year, a government raises so much in revenues (such as through taxation) and it spends another amount through its various departments (such as on health, education, defence, etc.). The government is able to influence the economic climate in a country by varying either or both of these sides of the fiscal equation.

Monetary policy is the regulation of the national economy by varying the supply and price of money. Money supply concerns the volume of money (in its various forms) in the economy and the 'price' of money is the base rate which determines the interest rate that banks and other lenders charge for borrowings.

In the UK, the Chancellor of the Exchequer is in charge of fiscal policy whilst monetary policy is overseen by the Monetary Policy Committee of the Bank of England.

When the effects of fiscal and monetary pressure work themselves out in the economy, they can affect any or all of the following economic factors:

- Economic growth rates (the year to year growth in the total size of a national economy, usually measured by gross domestic product).
- Levels of income in the economy.
- Levels of productivity (*i.e.* output per worker in the economy).
- Wage levels and the rate of increase in wages.
- Levels of inflation (*i.e.* the year to year rise in prices).
- Levels of unemployment.
- Balance of payments (a measure of the international competitiveness of one country's economy against its international; competitor countries).
- Exchange rates (the exchange value of one currency against another).

Economic growth, exchange rates, levels of income, inflation and unemployment will all affect people's ability to pay for goods and services and accordingly, they can affect levels and patterns of demand. Similarly, levels of productivity, wage levels, levels of inflation and exchange rates will affect costs of production and competitiveness. All of these indicators must be monitored in comparison to those faced by competitors abroad to provide indications of change in international competitiveness.

Economic Influences—airline sector

The economic environment of the airline sector has been characterized by growth in relation to most key figures. Air travel demand has closely mirrored the cyclical pattern shown by gross domestic product (GDP) figures in that it responds to cyclical upswings and downswings. However, air travel growth has far exceeded GDP growth over the period. Between 1960 and 1995 the total world economy, measured by GDP, grew by a factor of just over three, while air transport, measured by tonne-kilometres, grew by a factor of nearly 20 (Hanlon, 1999). The airline industry also has a high level of fixed costs and consequently average load factors and revenue measures per passenger are crucial in maintaining profitability. Furthermore, fuel and aircraft prices are major expenditure items subject to fluctuations and the international orientation of the industry means that movements in foreign exchange rates can have major effects upon industry profitability. Holloway (1998) maintained that aviation managers face the need to pursue strategies capable of sustaining profitability throughout entire economic cycles.

Environmental influences

The environmental influences here refer to the influence of concerns for the physical environment (both the natural environment and the built environment) on travel and tourism organizations. In recent years increasing concerns about ecology and 'green issues' has been an important social trend and this has changed people's attitudes towards the effects of products and operational processes on the environment. Issues such as global climate change, ozone layer depletion, deforestation, extinction of species, soil erosion, desertification, acid rain, toxic waster and water pollution have become important concerns with regard to the natural environment (Peattie and Moutinho, 2000). To such concerns regarding the natural environment might be added others concerning the built environment such as traffic congestion, deterioration buildings and historic sites, poor urban planning and visually inclusive buildings. The problems and issues identified have certain unifying characteristics. First, they all have international dimensions and second they are not exclusively tourism related but nevertheless have important implications for tourism managers amongst others.

Whereas twenty years ago most consumers showed little concern for the long-term effects of products and processes on the natural environment, today people are increasingly aware of the need to protect it. Following various developments such as the publication of the Brundtland Report in 1987 (WCED, 1987) and the Earth Summit in Rio de Janeiro in 1992, there has been increasing commitment to the principles of sustainable development in many industries, including tourism.

This has led to pressure on governments to introduce legislation and other measures to control pollution. The combined desire of consumers for products which are themselves environmentally friendly and which have been produced by 'green' methods has resulted in the realization by business that there are profits to be made by being environmentally friendly or at least appearing to be environmentally friendly. British Airways, for example, has developed a series of environmental awareness programmes for its managers and sponsored the 'Tourism for Tomorrow' awards in recognition of tourism organizations that have attempted to create products that have a positive environmental impact.

Scandic Hotels–environmental programme as a source of competitive advantage

Scandic Hotels (which is now part of Hilton plc.) is the leading hotel brand in Scandinavia, a region in which consumers traditionally are highly environmentally conscious. The group, which employs some 7500 people, has 155 hotels of which 133 are in the Scandinavian countries with others located around Europe. The brand, which positions itself as offering 'value for money', places great emphasis on continual competence development of employees at all levels of the organization and on its environmental programme.

Scandic's environmental programme was launched in 1994 following consultation with staff and the hotel group is an active member of the International Hotel Environment Initiative (IHEI). The programme involves the continuing education of all employees and includes initiatives such as:

- The introduction in 1995 of eco-rooms, which are 97% recyclable. More recently, the company has also developed 'eco-hotels', in which the entire construction of the hotels is guided by environmental principles. To date, more than 8000 eco-rooms and six eco-hotels have been built.
- The achievement of 'Swan' certification for four hotels. The Swan is the official eco-label in Scandinavia and verifies that the hotels have met stringent environmental standards.
- The abolition of individual soap and shampoo packages in 1994 reduced emissions of soap and shampoo by 40 metric tonnes and eliminated 10 million packages anuually.
- The introduction of the 'resource hunt', a programme promoting the efficient use of resources. Initially carried out in the Scandinavian hotels between 1997 and 1999, the programme reduced carbon dioxide emissions by more than 15% and energy costs by 20%.

During 2000, Scandic also introduced, following staff consultation, a community involvement programme called

'Scandic in Society' which aimed to define the company's role in society by engaging in local issues that were important to each community in which Scandic hotels were located. Through such a programme the company aimed to demonstrate its corporate citizenship and contribute to societal changes and improvements.

The issues of the sustainability of tourism development for tourist destinations and attractions has been widely addressed in the tourism literature over recent years by authors such as Hawkins and Holtz (2001), Weaver (2000), Berry and Ladkin (1997), Clarke (1997) and Mowforth and Munt (1998). A number of authors have also traced the environmental impacts of particular sectors of travel and tourism.

Graham (2001), for example, traced environamental policies and practices at a number of airports including Oslo, Manchester, London Heathrow and Amsterdam. Cartwright and Baird (1999) traced the environmental impacts of cruising and reported on the ways in which attempts have been made to reduce the polluting effect of cruise ships. The traditional method of removing rubbish from ships was to dump it overboard. Now such practices are outlawed and large fines are imposed on shipping companies found guilty of such pollution, partly in response to consumer pressures. A modern cruise ship such as P&O's *Oriana* contains four sewage plants so that as much rubbish as possible is retained and disposed of safely into containers at ports. There is also a worldwide ban on the discharge of fuel oil into the sea (Cartwright and Baird, 1999).

Environmental in influences—airline sector

Environmental concerns in the airline sector include the effects of noise and aircraft emissions and the impacts of developing airport and ground transportation infrastructure. Public tolerance of aircraft noise has been diminishing in spite of the reduction in noise levels due to the development of less noisy aircraft types (Graham, 2001). The problems associated with aircraft noise have led to ever more stringent and sophisticated noise abatement measures being introduced at most major airports. Some of these gases emitted by aircraft in flight, primarily carbon dioxide and water vapour, are greenhouse gases which contribute to global warming and climate change. However, it is thought that aviation's contribution to global human-made carbon dioxide emissions amounts to only around 2% of the total (Graham, 2001). The infrastructure of creating airports and ground transportation to support airlines has often proved controversial. Thus the agreement to proceed with a fifth terminal for London's Heathrow Airport was secured only after ten years of public consultations, whilst Manchester Airport proceeded with building a second runway in the face of strong lobbying by environmental pressure groups.

Political, governmental, legal and regulatory influences

The political environment is defined as that part of the macro-environment, which is under the direct control, or influence, of the government. Governments have direct control or influence over:

- *Legislation and regulation*—this covers laws that influence employment, consumer protection, health and safety at work, contract and trading, trade unions, monopolies and mergers, tax, etc.
- *Economic policy*—particularly over fiscal policy. Governments usually set policy over the levels of taxation and expenditure in the country.
- *Government-owned businesses*—nationslized industries. Some governments retain control over key strategic industries (such as airlines) and the way in which these are controlled can have 'knock-on' effects to other parts of the economy.

- *Government international policy*–government intervention to influence exchange rates, international trade, etc.

The objectives that a government may have towards the regulation of business will depend in large part upon the political leaning of the governing party. Most governments have, however, sought to construct policy over a number of key areas of business activity:

- Control of inflation (such as to improve international competitiveness).
- Promotion of economic growth and investment.
- Control of unemployment.
- Stabilization of exchange rates.
- Control of balance of payments.
- Control of monopoly power, both by businesses and trade unions.
- Provision of public and merit goods like health, education defence, etc.
- Control of pollution and environmental protection.
- Redistribution of incomes (to varying degrees).
- Consumer protection.
- Regulation of working conditions.
- Regulation of trade.

To varying degrees, all businesses will be affected by political influences. Accordingly, it is important for managers to monitor government policy to detect changes early so as to respond effectively.

Another important aspect of the political environment is *political risk* and its potential effects on business. Political risk is particularly important in international business. Whilst Western Europe and North America are comparatively politically stable, other parts of the world like Eastern Europe, South America, sub-Saharan Africa and parts of the Middle East have undergone periods of political instability. It is therefore necessary to monitor closely the political situation in these areas when trading with them, as the political risk are large. Even in more stable areas, political uncertainty can be higher at, for example, election times or when other political crises arise.

Political environment—airline sector

The political environment of the airline sector has been characterized by an extended network of national and international rules and regulations, many of which date back to the Chicago Convention of 1944 and the Bermuda Agreement of 1946 (Sampson, 1984). Based on the acknowledgment of the sovereignty of nations over their airspace and of the equal right for every nation to participate in air travel, the so-called *five freedoms of the air* were established:

- *First Freedom*—The right to fly over another country without landing.
- *Second Freedom*—The right to make a landing for technical reasons (*e.g.* refuelling) in another country without picking up/setting down revenue traffic.
- *Third Freedom*—The right to carry revenue traffic from your own country (A) to the country (B) of your treaty partner.
- *Fourth Freedom*—The right to carry revenue traffic from country B back to your own country A.
- *Fifth Freedom*—The right of an airline from country A to carry revenue traffic between country B and other countries such as C or D on services starting or ending in its home country A. (The freedom cannot be used unless countries C or D also agree.)

(Source: Doganis, 2001)

The five freedoms were followed by a complex web of bilateral inter-governmental agreements that allowed national governments involved to maintain control over national interests related to air travel. A more liberal approach is reflected in the so called *open skies* agreements granting carriers of the states involved unlimited access to the routes between airports in these states. The concept of open skies reflects a development of major importance for the airline industry: liberalization unfolding around the globe (Doganis, 2001).

In the USA (which accounts for over 40% of the world's airline industry), the strict regulations governing the domestic air travel market were swept away by the Airline Deregulation Act of 1978. The act abolished regulations specifying the carriers that were allowed to fly on particular routes and impose controls on air fares. After deregulation many new carriers entered the market (and many subsequently folded), but most of the largest carriers, such as United, American, Dalta and Northwest, survived but undoubtedly competition in the US domestic market has increased in the longer term by the emergence of low cost carriers such as Southwest Airlines.

Subsequently, similar deregulation occurred in Europe. A different approach towards implementation was selected, however, owing to the complexity of achieving deregulation in the fragmented political landscape of the European Union. Consequently, a step by step process towards liberalization took place which culminated in 1997. Another major trend among European governments was the privatization (in whole or in part) of former state-owned carriers such as British Airways, Air France and Lufthansa.

Heavy regulation over the ownership of airlines remains, however. In many cases, such as the USA, airlines must still be 'substantially owned' or effectively controlled by nationals of the designated states. Thus airlines continue to be treated in a different manner to most other industries, reflecting its strategic significance and as Doganis (2001) pointed out, paradoxically the most internatonal of industries remains almost exclusively national in terms of ownership and control.

The relationships between the STEEP influences

The example of environmental influences

A temptations when carrying out a STEEP analysis is to think of each influence as separate when in fact they are often interlinked. The effects of environmental influences on organization provide an example. The environmental concerns themselves (such as the use of water resources for golf course developments or the building of visually intrusive hotels in scenic areas) are issues to be dealt with within the 'environmental' category of the STEEP analysis. However, such concerns might also involve social, political and technological factors in the analysis. Thus, social factors (increased awareness) have impacted on political factors (legislation and regulation) and the two forces together have produced technological change (products and processes which are less damaging to the environment). Accordingly, a macro-environmental analysis should recognize the ways in which the four STEEP factors might be linked to each other.

Using the STEEP analysis

How to carry out a STEEP analysis

Now that we know what the STEEP influences are and how they are interrelated, we turn to actually using the framework in strategic analysis. The analysis is generally considered as falling into four stages:

1. Scanning and monitoring the macro-environment for actual or potential changes in social, technological, economic and political factors.
2. Assessing the relevance and importance of the changes for the market, industry and business.
3. Analysing each of the relevant changes in detail and the potential relationships between them.
4. Assessing the potential impact of the changes on the market, industry and business.

What to analyse

When managers carry out a STEEP analysis as part of a strategic analysis (and the same is true of students examine a case study), they would normally examine how each factor might impact upon :

- *The internal parts of the organization*–the effects of STEEP factors on the organization's core competences, strategies, resources and value system.
- *An organization's markets*– the effects of STEEP factors on product markets (*e.g.* market size, structure, segments, customer wants, etc.) and resource markets.
- *The industry in which the organization competes*– the effects of STEEP factors on the five competitive forces.

❑❑❑

Bibliography

Argenti, J. (1997) Stakeholders: the Case Against. *Long Range Planning,* 30(3), 442-445.

Athiyaman, A. (1995) The Interface of Tourism and Strategy Research an Analysis. *Tourism Management,* 16(6), 447-453.

Athiyaman, A. and Robertson, R.W. (1995) Strategic Planning in Large Tourism Firms: an Empirical Analysis. *Tourism Management,* 16(3), 199-205.

Baetz, M.C. and Bart, C.K. (1996) Developing Mission Statements Which Work, *Long Range Planning,* 29(4), 526-533.

Bart, C.K. (1997) Sex, Lies and Mission Statements. *Business Horizons,* November-December.

Berry, S. and Ladkin, A (1997) Sustainable Tourism: a Regional Perspective. *Tourims Management,* 18 (7), 433–40.

British Airways News (1987) To be the Undisputed Leader in World Travel. No. 1158, 2 May.

Buhalis, D., (2001) The Tourist Phenomenon: The New Tourist and Consumer, in S. Wahab and C. Cooper (eds), *Tourism in the Age of Globalisation.* London: Routledge.

Brown, S.F. (2001) How to Build a Really Big Plane. *Fortune.* No. 5, pp. 76-82.

Cartwright, R. and Baird, C. (1999) *The Development and Growth of the Cruise Industry.* Oxford: Butterworth-Heinemann.

Chakravarthy, B. (1997) A New Strategy Framework for Coping with Turbulence. *Sloan Management Review,* Winter, pp. 69–82.

Chandler, A.D. (1962), *Strategy and Structure.* Boston, MA : MIT Press.

Charke, J. (1997) A Framework of Approaches to Sustainable Tourism. *Journal of Sustainable Tourism,* 5(3), 224–233.

Cooper, C. and Gilbert, D. (1998) Models and Patterns of Tourism Demand, in C. Cooper, J. Fletcher, D. Gilbert, R. Shepherd and S. Wanhill, *Tourism Principles and Practice.* Harlow: Longman.

David, E.R. (1989) How Companies Define Their Mission. *Long Range Planning,* 22(1), 90-97.

Dev, C.S. (1989) Operating Environment and Strategy: the Profitable Connection. *Cornell Hotel and Restaurant Administration Quarterly,* 30(2), 9-14.

Doganis, R. (2001) *The Airline Business in the 21st Century. London:* Routledge.

Donaldson, T. and Preston, L.E. (1995). The Stakeholder Theory of the Corporation: Concepts, Evidence, and Implications. *Academy of Management Review,* 20, 65-91.

Elenkov, D.E. (1997) Strategic Uncertainty and Environmental Scanning: the Case for Institutional Influences on Scanning Behaviour. *Strategic management Journal,* 18(4), 287–302.

Ellis, J. and Williams, D. (1993) *Corporate Strategy and Financial Analysis.* London : Pitman.

Evans, N. (2002) Financial Management in Travel and

Tourism, in Sharpley, R. (ed.) *The Tourism Business*, 2nd edn. Sunderland: Business Education Publishers.

Fahey, L. and Narayanan, V.K. (1986) *Macro-environment* Analysis for Strategic management. St. Paul, MN: West Publishing.

Franks, J. R. and Broyles, J.E. (1979) *Modern Managerial Finance.* London: John Wiley.

Ginter, P. and Duncan, J. (1990) Macro-environmental Analysis. *Long Range Planning,* December.

Graham, A. (2001) *Managing Airports: an International Perspective.* Oxford: Butterworth-Heinemann.

Hanlon, P. (1999) *Global Airlines,* 2nd edn. Oxford: Butterworth-Heinemann.

Hawkins, D.E. and Holtz, C. (2001) Environmental Policies and Management Systems Related to the Global Tourism Industry, in S. Wahab and C. Cooper (eds), *Tourism in the Age of Globalization.* London: Routledge.

Helms, M.M. and Wright, P. (1992) External Considerations: Their Influence on Future Strategic Planning. *Management Decision,* 30(8), 4–11.

Holloway, S. (1998) *Changing Planes: A Strategic Management Perspective on an Industry in Transition.* Aldershot: Ashgate.

Johnson, G. and Scholes, K. (2002) *Exploring Corporate Strategy.* Harlow: Pearson Education.

Kandampully, J. and Duddy, R. (2001) Service System: A Strategic Approach to Gain a Competitive Advantage in the Hospitality and Tourism Industry. *International Journal of Hospitality and Tourism Administration,* 2(1), 27-47.

Kaplan. R. S. and Norton, D.P. (2001) *The Strategy Focused Organisation.* Boston, MA: Harvard Business School Press.

Kay, J. (1995) Learning to Define the Core Business. *Financial Times,* 1 December.

Kay, J. (1993) *Foundations of Corporate Success.* Oxford: Oxford University Press.

Levitt, T. (1983) The Globalisation of Markets. *Harvard Business Review,* May/June.

Lockwood, A. and Medlik, S. (2001) *Tourism and Hospitality in the 21st Century.* Oxford: Butterworth-Heinemann.

Lynch, R. (2000) *Corporate Strategy,* 2nd edn. Harlow: Pearson Education.

Makridakis, S. (1990) *Forecasting, Planning, and strategy for the 21st Century.* New York: Free Press.

Mintzberg, II. (1991) *The Strategy Process Concepts, Contexts, Cases.* Englewood Cliffs, NJ: Prentice Hall.

Moutinho, I. (ed.) (2000) *Strategic Management in Tourism.* Wallingford: CABI.

Mowforth, M. and Munt, I. (1998) *Tourism and Stustainability: New Tourism in the Third World.* London: Routledge.

Nickson, D. (2000) Human Resource Issues in Travel and Tourism, in L. Moutinho (ed.), *Strategic Management in Tourism.* Walling-ford: CABI, pp. 169-185.

Olsen, M.D. (1991) Strategic Management in the Hospitality Industry: a Literature Review. *Progress in Tourism, Recreation and Hospitality Management,* 3, 215-231.

Olsen, M.D., West, J. and Tse, E.C. (1998) *Strategic Management in the Hospitality Industry,* 2nd edn. New ork: John Wiley.

Owen, G. (1998) *Accounting for Hospitality, Tourism and Leisure,* 2nd edn. Harlow: Longman.

Peattie, K. and Moutinho, L. (2000) The marketing environment for travel and tourism, in L. Moutinho (ed). *Strategic Management in Tourism.* Wallingford: CABI.

Poon, A (1993) *Tourism Technology and Competitive Strategies.* Wallingford: CABI.

Reichheld, F.E. and Sasser, W.E. (1990) Zero Defections: Quality Comes to Services. *Harvard Business Review,*

September/October, 105-111.

Reichhheld, F.E. and Sasser, W.E. (1990) Zero Defections: Quality Comes to Services. *Harvard Business Review*, September/October, 105-111.

Riley, M. (1996) *Human Resource Management in the Hospitality and Tourism Industry*. Oxford: Butterworth Heinemann.

Ross, D.A. (1996) *International Treasury management,* 3rd edn. London: Euromoney Publications.

Ryan, C. (1996) Market Research in Tourism: Shifting Paradigms for New Concerns, in L. Moutinho (ed.), *Marketing Research in Tourism.* London: Prentic Hall.

Sampson, A. (1984) *Empires of the Sky: The politics, Contests and Cartets of world Airlines.* London: Hodder and Stoughton.

Sanchez, R. (1995) Strategic Flexibility. From Organization and Managerial Work in Dynamic Markets: A Strategic Options Perspective. *Advances in Strategic Management,* 9, 251–91.

Sanchez. R. (1995) Strategic Flexibility in Product Competition, *Strategic Management Journal,* 16 (Summer), 135-159.

Stonehouse, G.H., Hamill, J. and Purdie, A. (1999) *Global and Transnational Business Strategy and Management.* London: John Wiley.

Strebel, P. (1992) *Breakpoints.* Cambridge, MA: Harvard Business School Press.

The Economist (2001) Gilbert Trigano [Club Med founder] Obituary, 10 February, p. 129.

Turner, I. (1996) Working with Chaos. *Financial Times,* 4 October.

Teare, R. and Boer, R. (1991) *Strategic Hospitality Management.* London: Cassell.

Tribe, J. (1997) *Corporate Strategy for Tourism.* London: International Thomson Business Press, ch. 2.

Vanhove, N. (2001) Globalisation of Tourism Demand, Global Distribution Systems and Marketing, in S. Wahab and C. Cooper (eds), *Tourism in the Age of Globalisation*. London: Routledge.

Vogel, H.L. (2001) *Travel Industry Economics*. Cambridge: Cambridge University Press.

WCED (World Commission on Environment and Development) (1987) *Our Common Future*. Oxford University Press.

Weaver, D. (2000) Sustainable Tourism: Is it Sustainable, in B. Faulkner, G. Moscardo and E. Laws (eds), *Tourism in the 21st Century: Lessons from Experience*. London: Continuum.

www.scandic-hotels.com

□□□